D1547535

"MR. McCAMEY"
CLAUDE W. BROWN

The Life of a Texas Oil Man

By
Robert Nash
and
Peggy Nichols Nash

EAKIN PRESS ★ Austin, Texas

Copyright © 1994
By Robert Nash
and
Peggy Nichols Nash

Published in the United States of America
By Eakin Press
A Division of Sunbelt Media, Inc.

ISBN 0-89015-976-9

10 9 8 7 6 5 4 3 2

Library of Congress Cataloging-in-Publication Data:

Nash, Robert.
    Mr. McCamey — Claude W. Brown : life of a west Texas oil man / by
Robert Nast and Peggy Nichols Nash. — 1st ed.
    p.   cm.
    Includes bibliographical references and index.
    ISBN 0-89015-976-9 : $15.95
    1. Brown, Claude Wilson, 1904–1993. 2. Industrialists — Texas — Biogra-
phy. 3. Petroleum industry and trade — United States — History. I. Nash,
Peggy Nichols. II. Title.
HD9570.B76A3   1995
338.2'7282'092 — dc20
[B]   94-37570
                                                                        CIP

Contents

Foreword

Claude W. Brown was more than "Mr. McCamey." His vision encompassed the entire Permian Basin. All of us in the region benefited from his wisdom, work, and enthusiasm.

Colonel Brown was a solid booster of our area. He contributed time, money, and political influence to enrich the many educational, health, and cultural opportunities available to West Texans. He helped organize and support the West Texas Chamber of Commerce, the Permian Basin Petroleum Museum, the University of Texas of the Permian Basin, the Presidential Museum, Texas Tech University Health Sciences Center Medical School in Odessa, and the Midland-Odessa Symphony, to name only a few.

I first knew Colonel Brown through my employers, W. D. Noel and E. G. Rodman, Sr., who also made their mark in the oil fields of McCamey. When former Attorney General John Ben Shepperd joined Noel and Rodman, their close friendship through the Democratic Party cemented the relationship. It was John Ben who conferred the honorary "Colonel in the Texas Navy" to Claude Brown, and we always called him that out of respect and admiration.

Robert and Peggy Nash capture the true Claude Brown — a gentleman in both word and deed. He brought integrity and kindness to a business often bereft of both. His word was his bond and his leadership unquestioned. People followed him because he always worked for the best interests of his family, employees, neighbors, and community.

I commend the Nashes for their excellent portrayal not only of this esteemed man but also of the oil field environment of

West Texas. Their depiction of the booms and busts, the risks and rewards, is accurate and exciting.

As one with a lifelong interest in history, especially of this area, I recommend this narrative. It captures the feel and atmosphere of the oil patch and traces its evolution into a giant industry.

Reading about Claude Brown's part in its development is to learn about the best of the oil men. Thousands of fortune seekers passed through this area, but Colonel Brown and those of his caliber stayed to build communities. West Texas is grateful that he chose to call McCamey and the Permian Basin his home.

— GRACE KING
Charter member, Permian Historical Society,
and Chairman, Heritage of Odessa Foundation

Preface

Claude Brown was born on a Texas farm four years after Spindletop ushered in a new age for the state of Texas. His first job after graduating from high school in 1922 was as a roustabout in the wide-open Mexia field. For the next seventy-one years he was an oil man.

This is his story.

Claude W. Brown

The Top Hand Award is a salute and an expression of gratitude, recognition and respect to Claude W. Brown, who for sixty-six years has worked in and served the independent petroleum industry as a finder and producer of oil. The award is a symbol of admiration for his legendary record as a pioneer of the Permian Basin oil industry, as a founding father and former president of the Permian Basin Petroleum Association and in honor of his commitment as a loving husband and father and as a civic leader who has devoted his time and financial support freely toward the cause of community and educational enhancement and family tranquility. For his significant contributions to petroleum industry and community excellence and his unswerving commitment to family and friends, Claude W. Brown is named the Permian Basin Petroleum Association's Top Hand for 1988.

PRESENTED BY P.B.P.A. AT ITS 26TH ANNUAL MEETING
MIDLAND, TEXAS
AUGUST 19, 1988

Acknowledgments

Every book is the result of many contributors, and this book is no exception. We owe special gratitude to Betty Orbeck of the Permian Basin Petroleum Museum; Bill Collyns of Midland, a resident of McCamey in the 1930s; Nancy McCall of Midland; Kay Rochelle Williams, director of the Mendoza Trail Museum in McCamey; Brenda Mitchell; C. C. Carll, publisher of *The McCamey News*; and Ed Todd and the editorial staff of the *Midland Reporter-Telegram*. Most material in this book is based on interviews with Mr. Brown, on his personal papers, and on talks with members of the Brown family.

In later years of his life, Claude Brown was a frequent speaker for civic and petroleum-industry groups.

Roustabout from McCamey

He held them in the palm of his hand. Slender and shrewd, a bit of a showman and every inch an entrepreneur, he focused pale blue eyes on his audience and explained how oil is found in the real world.

He spoke of up-dips and anticlines, of overrides and Christmas trees, frac tanks and farmouts, well logs and wet oil and widow makers: the everyday, exotic language of the wildcatter.

Words and phrases his listeners had learned on a theoretical level rolled from his lips with the ease of usage. He also used terms they had not heard; a definite and formidable gap existed between their academic training and his school of hard knocks.

To a man, they were products of the proud schools that specialize in turning out leaders of the oil and gas industry: the University of Texas, the University of Oklahoma, Texas A&M, Tulsa University, Louisiana State University. Young and highly educated engineers, they had but a few years' experience in the Permian Basin.

In the south ballroom of Midland's elegant burgundy and marble Petroleum Club, the industry's new hands had gathered to hear an elder statesman tell his story. It was October 1972.

Claude Wilson Brown had taken the floor.

The wiry West Texan obligingly reminisced on his fifty highly motivated and superbly self-reliant years in the oil patch, from roughnecking to selling pipe to drilling wells. His efforts, together with a rising market, had made him an influential member of the oil industry. He had seen times so hard that he shot jackrabbits on the halves with a borrowed shotgun; ultimately, he gave away millions.

Were there any questions? He looked politely around the room.

"Mr. Brown." An earnest young engineer stood in the third row. "Sir, in view of all you have accomplished in the oil patch with your, er, background — where do you suppose you would be today if you had had a college degree?"

Brown's face crinkled in a smile. The keen eyes twinkled.

"Why, I guess I'd be out there with you boys, drawing a paycheck. Listening to somebody else up here, telling me how to do it."

Soon the mild-mannered man who called himself "just a roustabout from McCamey" finished his remarks and headed for home.

Through dry brown hardpan a fifty-four-mile ribbon of concrete, most of it straight as a ruler, connects Midland and McCamey. It is an open, empty land, baked by centuries of sun, the horizon visible in every direction; no sign of movement but the walking beams of oil well pumps, bent like calves at a feed trough. For centuries this land was hunted over, grazed over, and fought over, but never broken. Sagebrush and tumbleweed country, its arid surface concealing unseen depths wet with oil.

Driving south on Highway 349, Brown's mind might have replayed images of the past.

Life had been quite a ride, from the hand-to-mouth days of the Depression — when he worked for a dollar a day and was glad to get it — to the Petroleum Club in 1972.

His journey began in a horse-drawn wagon. It took the Brown family thirty days in 1908 to travel from Ballinger to the Gulf Coast. Today, one makes the trip in an hour by jet.

Henry Ford's invention of the Model-T changed everything. Overnight, oil was the essential commodity. The Permian Basin became as crucial to oil as Detroit is to the automobile. West Texas crude oil later proved to be a critical factor in the Allied victory in World War II.

Claude Brown was one of the few dozen inventive, pragmatic men who played key roles in the development of the oil-rich Permian Basin.

Fascinating business, this search for oil. It got in your blood.

Oil was a jealous mistress; it could clean a man out, leave him broke, then seduce him to come back begging for more. Hope died hard. The odds were against him, but in the Permian Basin a wildcatter just might be the right man in the right place at the right time. He might emulate Odysseus, ancient Greek archetype for all time of a man who has battled the storms of life and won.

This vast, unforgiving land once lay at the bottom of an inland sea. Scientists believe that this part of Texas formed ocean beds during the Permian Age 240 million years ago. Forty such basins have been identified in the continental United States. The Permian, which includes several smaller basins, is the largest.

Incredibly, farms of cotton and wheat, and ranches of goats and cattle, had once consisted of primeval ooze that sustained life in snails and sea ferns. The Permian Basin today is still a sea, the wine-dark sea of adventure; the wildcatter, like Odysseus, yet sails the voyage of discovery.

CHAPTER ONE

The Berry Clan

"Oh God, it is all over!" Lord North exclaimed when word reached him of Cornwallis' surrender at Yorktown. The American Revolution had ended only a few miles from Jamestown, where America had begun in 1607.[1]

Nearly two million people lived in the young nation when the fighting stopped in 1781. Philadelphia, with a population of 35,000, was getting too crowded for comfort. The new American turned his face west. Scotch-Irish pioneers and their horses and cattle, wives and children, converged on the roads to Pittsburgh and streamed through the Cumberland Gap into Kentucky. Lexington and Concord gave way in the American psyche to continental expansion.

While frontiersmen pushed through the Appalachians, American commissioners in Paris were negotiating the peace treaty. The strange trio of John Adams, John Jay, and Benjamin Franklin, diverse in most ways, together had the "unconscious feel of the continent, the continental will, that shaped a demand."[2] In the Treaty of Paris the three set a precedent that held for American diplomacy until the U.S. evacuated Saigon in 1975: they got more than there was any realistic expectation the United States would be able to get. They got the entire West, all the way to the Mississippi River.

The Scotch-Irish clans had turned their backs on Europe in the eighteenth century and sailed in droves to America. This vanguard had no armies or heroes, but it constituted a force that would leave its indelible stamp on American culture. Tired of popes, they rejected the medieval panoply of mystery and pageantry and embraced the teachings of Calvin and Knox. Function became more important than status. Aristocrats were superfluous; beggars were to be despised. With the East Coast torn by factions of Federalists and Republicans after 1783, the Scotch-Irish clans began America's love affair with the middle class.

The French historian De Riencourt described these strange folk:

> Strong, inhumanly self-reliant . . . these puritans were geared for a life of action. They shunned . . . contemplation and determined to throw their fanatical energy into the struggle against Nature . . . brushing aside all men who stood in their path.[3]

New Englanders disliked the Scotch-Irish, finding them unruly and poverty-stricken. "These confounded Irish," complained the surveyor general of Boston, "will eat us all up."[4]

The clans then headed for Philadelphia, known for religious toleration and its resultant prosperity. Pennsylvanians welcomed the Scots as a buffer against the French and the Indians.

Pugnacious and loyal, the Scots never dodged a fight. Historian William MacNeil said they became the shock troops in the American Revolution and accounted for half the rebel army. Sixty years later, in a Texas dawn, they would man most of the guns at the Alamo.

Arnold Toynbee has written that men born in the middle border in the late eighteenth and early nineteenth centuries were probably the toughest, and toughest-minded, in American history. These frontiersmen were blessed with the skills they would need for the struggle. They were not afraid of work; they were not afraid of war. The Anglo-Saxons had long-term goals, and they were immensely adaptive in reaching them. They had the organizational skills of European civilization—possibly their greatest heritage—and they had the sense of order of the English-speaking peoples. With their axes and Bibles, their rusty fiddles and long-barreled rifles, the Anglo-Saxons headed west to forge a new cosmos.

Along the way, in 1786, Claude Brown's Texas ancestor, John

Berry, was born in West Louisville, Kentucky. He served in the spy company of the Kentucky militia in the War of 1812. Around 1810 Berry married Betsy Smothers, who gave birth to three sons: Joseph, John Bate, and Andrew Jackson (Jack). Betsy died about 1819.[5]

In May 1826 John Berry and his second wife, Gracie Treat, and their three daughters (as well as John and Betsy's three sons) moved to Texas. Mexico granted Berry one of the original town lots in Liberty. There Berry opened a blacksmith shop. His sons Bate and Jack fought with Gen. Sam Houston at San Jacinto.

Joe and Bate joined the ill-fated Mier Expedition to Mexico in 1842. Joe was bayoneted; Bate was taken prisoner and released from Perote prison in 1844.

In August 1845 Berry received a land grant of a league and a labor (4,605 acres) three miles northeast of Georgetown, in the rolling hills of what is now Williamson County. Six more children, including two sets of twins, were born on the Berry League.

Hannah Berry, second daughter of John Berry and Gracie Treat, married Moses Hughes in 1840. Seeking medicinal sulphur waters fifty miles west, Moses and Hannah Hughes became the first white settlers in Lampasas. Hannah died, at the age of forty, giving birth to her twelfth child.[6]

Moses and Hannah's son Wilson became the grandfather of Claude Wilson Brown.

Hughes Springs flowed at the rate of two to three million gallons of water a day. A hundred years later, in boomtown McCamey, Claude Brown would pay one dollar a barrel for drinking water. When he did, he thought of the two-story rock home in which his grandfather grew up. He remembered going there in a surrey with his mother; seeing the burro tied at the hitching post to warn of Indian attack. He remembered the clear spring water. Would he ever see a mineral flow that fast again?

CHAPTER TWO

The Division Order

Texas began the twentieth century much as it had entered the Union in 1845: a remote land, beguiling and harsh, with sparse population and a strong sense of separatism. Land was the reason for Texas and land was its continuing source of wealth: first, with the great cotton plantations; next, with the cattle industry after 1865; then the timber empires; and finally, the oil boom.[1]

The state's rigid sense of privacy produced the strongest trespass laws of any state in the Union. Its notion of private right was, paradoxically, best expressed not by a Texan but by New Englander Emily Dickinson:

> The soul selects her own society,
> Then shuts the door. . . .[2]

Texans might have preferred to let the rest of the world go by, but the world had already become too small. The nation's problems eventually would percolate into Texas. Hard money, tight credit, drought, banks, and foreclosures had by 1900 caused more heartache than the Mexican wars or Indian raids of the preceding century.

Into this world Claude Wilson Brown was born December 7, 1904.

Claude's mother was Hattie Lee Hughes, granddaughter of Moses and Hannah Hughes. Born at the family home in Hughes Springs, near Lampasas, Hattie Lee Hughes married Thomas P.

Claude Brown's parents with their infant daughter, Ada. (Circa 1900, Balinger.)

Brown and gave birth to six children: Ada, Tom, Ruby, Claude, Homer, and Marion.

When Claude was six months old, Thomas Brown quit his job with the Santa Fe railroad at Talpa. He traded for eighty acres of cotton land and moved his family to the New Home community near Winters.

Thomas Brown developed catarrh, a throat inflammation that provoked a chronic nosebleed. Uncontrollable bleeding at times caused him to faint. His doctor prescribed a change in climate: the Gulf Coast.

Brown prepared for the trip by building a covered wagon with a cook box on the back. Mr. and Mrs. Norvell, neighbors in Winters, decided to join the Brown family. They traveled in their own covered wagon. An old bachelor, Mr. Plummer, joined the caravan in a hack with covered top and one horse.

The travelers covered twenty miles a day. At sundown they would set up camp, cook supper in a Dutch oven, and stake the horses in a bar ditch so they could graze at night.

"Averaging twenty miles a day, it took us thirty days to make the six-hundred-mile trip," Claude said. "I made the same trip sixty years later in a Lear jet with my friend Bobby French in forty-five minutes. But I enjoyed it more as a four-year-old."

The Brown family stayed a year in Rockport. Two years later they made the same trip, again for their father's health. On the second trip Ruby Brown, Claude's oldest sister, contracted typhoid fever. The family stopped at Sinton, rented a house, and stayed there a month until Ruby was well. Sinton later became headquarters for Plymouth Oil Company; Claude Brown would drill thirty to forty oil wells for the company in Crockett County.

In Rockport, Ruby celebrated her sixteenth birthday and Claude entered first grade.

Salt air and sea breezes improved Thomas Brown's health. In 1916 the family returned to Ballinger. Thomas Brown traded his eighty-acre cotton farm for a twenty-acre fruit farm near Winters that produced peaches, plums, pears, apricots, and blackberries.

The six Brown children worked on the farm every day; they also managed to stay in school. In good weather they walked two miles to the two-room school. When roads were muddy they rode a donkey.

Claude came home one afternoon late in 1916 and handed his mother a letter from the RFD box. Hattie Lee Brown placed the letter on the round oak dining table.

"Open it, Mama. The letter's addressed to you."

Hattie Lee shrugged. "You open it."

Claude took out his pocketknife and slit the envelope. His eyes raced over the pages; he sank into a chair. The boy looked up.

"Mama? What's a division order?"

"Well, Hattie Lee." Lawyer O. L. Parish looked over his rimless spectacles at Mrs. Brown, her children standing behind her chair. Parish's office on the courthouse square in Ballinger smelled of tobacco and linseed oil. "What you've got here is a division order."

"A division order? What does it mean?"

"A division order is a contract of sale to the purchaser of oil or gas."

"Why did it come to me?"

"It came to you because you've inherited some mineral rights in Oklahoma. Pretty nice surprise, I'd say."

"I don't know who I would inherit them from."

"You inherited them from Moses Hughes. He owned minerals on a piece of Indian land near Madill, Oklahoma. The rights passed on to Moses Hughes' son, Enoch Hughes, and then to you. Clear as a bell. They belong to you now."

"Moses Hughes! My grandfather! I never knew him, and I haven't heard his name since I was five years old."

"They say God rewards the righteous, Hattie Lee." Parish looked pleased and a bit puzzled. "Just sign on this line. And this one on the next page."

Hattie Lee looked around expectantly. "Claude . . ."

"Here, Mama, let me. I'll sign it for you."

The first oil check reached Hattie Lee thirty days later. Excited children watched her open the envelope and pull out a check for seventeen hundred dollars.

"We bought our first Model-T," Claude recalled. "Paid four hundred fifty dollars for it. We had to hand-crank it and use curtains on the windows if it rained. It was more than we had ever had or hoped to have."

After the first check, the monthly oil income was about $175 until the minerals played out in 1921. The princely sum of $175 was enough to enable all the Brown children to stay in school until they graduated.

Brown remembered his mother's teasing: "Your papa's in bad health, but he always feels like walking a quarter of a mile to the mailbox on the day the oil check comes."

"Seventy-five years later it's still a kick," Brown grinned. "Getting the oil check once a month."

About the time of Claude Brown's birth, in 1904, two events occurred that would define the century.

In England a mechanic named Henry Royce formed a British company known as Royce, Ltd. It would manufacture and sell the Rolls-Royce motor car, a vehicle of mechanical excellence.

In America on June 16, 1905, the motor car designed by mechanic Henry Ford observed its first birthday. This anniversary signified that Ford Motor Company might have survived the dreadful infant-mortality rate then prevalent among start-up companies in the young automobile industry.

The life and times of Brown's generation were molded by these events. Henry Ford brought out his Model-T in 1908. It shook, rattled, and rolled on and on to become the most famous car of all times. The Model-T was produced for twenty years before Henry Ford would allow the design to be changed.

Above all, the Model-T was cheap. It put the nation on wheels and wrought a social phenomenon. For the first time in history, the non-rich became mobile. Only the wealthy could afford a Rolls-Royce; anyone who had a job could buy a Model-T.

The mass market created by the Model-T – and its use of the assembly line, which was immediately copied by competitors – brought an enormous demand for gasoline. Manufacturing cars, and building roads for their use, powered the U.S. economy through the first three decades of the century. Industrial growth meant oil; much of that oil was to be found in Texas.

The first hole in Texas earth drilled in search of oil was a 106-foot well dug by Lynis T. Barrett near Nacogdoches in 1866.

Rancher George Dullnig, drilling for water in 1889 on his land six miles southeast of San Antonio, struck oil at 235 feet. Disappointed, he moved fifteen feet and sank another well. Again, he struck oil rather than water. A third well also failed to produce water. The fourth well, northwest of the other three, produced gas, which Dullnig used as fuel. His yield of forty-eight barrels of oil, plus gas, put Texas into the 1889 federal census as an oil/gas producer.

Serious exploration began in Texas. Eventually, one well near Beaumont would change everything. On the sharp cold morning of January 10, 1901, a gusher blew in at 75,000 to 80,000 barrels a day. Capt. Anthony Lucas had not just completed a well; he had introduced the state of Texas to the industrial age. First cotton, then cattle; finally, oil. Texas was changed forever by Spindletop.

In the 1920s oil checks began appearing in a line moving steadily west from the 100th meridian. Farm and ranch communities in West Texas, plagued by drought in 1916–1918 and still reeling from the Depression of 1893, welcomed the chaotic new industry. The payroll of an oil company could insure financial survival to struggling rural towns.

The oil bonanza caught on like wildfire. Boomtowns popped up from the Panhandle to the lower Permian Basin. Some, like Ranger and Snyder, developed from existing rural communities. Ranger's population jumped from 700 to 50,000. Both Burkburnett and Breckenridge grew from 300 to more than 20,000.[3] McCamey and Borger, by contrast, appeared full-blown, like Venus; they sprang up almost overnight and depended entirely on income from oil fields. Saloons, dance halls, and gambling were the order of the day, every day and night. Courtesy was endemic, as it always had been in Texas; the penalty for discourtesy was violent. Vigilante committees dispensed justice. The revolver represented authority.

Wildcatters cared not that the odds were against them. Texas has always attracted men willing to give odds, since Coronado marched north across the Rio Grande 400 years ago in search of fabled cities of gold.

The old aristocracy in Texas had used tools of rope and plow and branding iron; the new aristocracy would use tools of capital and technology. The new breed of aristocrats would not always have a lot of money, but they would learn how to get capital and how to use it. They had the courage to back their own judgment, to play their cards with a steady hand.

CHAPTER THREE

Promoters

If his cousin Robert Woods had not been so tenderhearted, Claude Brown might not have gone to the oil fields.

In September 1918 Robert, two years older than Claude and his classmate in school, applied for a part-time job delivering telegrams. Every boy in town considered the job a prize, and Robert was in a strategic position to win it because his sister was being courted by the manager of Western Union in Ballinger. (She later married him.)

World War I was grinding into its bloody climax, with the inevitable messages of sons and husbands killed or wounded in action. Sixteen-year-old Robert felt emotionally shattered when he delivered a telegram edged in black.

Robert wanted moral support. He persuaded Claude, fourteen at the time, to go with him. Claude rode the rear seat of a two-seater bike. One day the boys came across a sight that intrigued them.

Two miles west of Ballinger, promoters calling themselves Safety First Oil Company drilled an exploratory well. Safety First had not only a drilling rig in operation; it had a publicity booth as well, only a few feet away from the rig. Telegraph wires in the booth could send and receive messages anywhere in the nation. Most of them went to California. Against the insistent grind of drilling, half a dozen men shouted: "Any minute! It's any minute now! She's going to blow in any minute!"

Robert and Claude liked to slow their bike on the dirt road and take in the spectacle. Claude could sense what was happen-

14

ing—that certain gullible Californians were being separated from their money.

Claude Brown wrote years later that while his mother's royalty income had been his first oil-related experience, Safety First was his first view of an oil promotion.

Oil man David Duncan could smell promoters before he could see them: "Promoters moved in. They would buy acreage, up to ten thousand dollars for an acre. They would form a company and sell off one million dollars worth of stock, then start a well.

"Maybe they would get a little well. They would get all the money they wanted because it didn't cost over fifty thousand dollars to drill a well and put it in a tank.

"There must have been a hundred of them drilled that way. Promoters got money from honest people from all over the United States. They really had a racket going! It was absolutely pitiful the way they took the public."[1]

The Safety First well came in a dry hole, naturally. A few individuals went to jail, while their colleagues rolled on to greener pastures, financed by California investors.

As Safety First was leaving town, word of high wages in the Ranger oil fields filtered back to Ballinger.

The Ranger oil strike began October 17, 1917, when McCleskey No. 1 roared in with an initial production rate of 1,700 barrels a day. Timing of the well could not have been more critical historically. With the U.S. committed to war, the nation needed large and immediate supplies of oil. In less than two years, the Ranger field produced two million barrels of oil a month. The field yielded high-grade oil that sold for $2.60 a barrel in 1917 and $4.25 a barrel in 1918.

After the Ranger strike, another huge gusher was brought in at the nearby community of Hogtown (later changed to Desdemona). Duke No. 1 came in at an incredible 10,000 to 15,000 barrels a day, albeit for a short play. Street talk said backers of Duke No. 1 received $26,000 for each dollar invested in the well.

More fields opened in North and Central Texas: Eastland, Cisco, Wichita Falls, Breckenridge, Mexia. Production and distribution were clearly in their infant stages, but the nation's expanding industrial machine demanded fuel.

In 1920 Texas production ranked third in the nation, with

the Permian Basin and East Texas fields yet to be discovered. The war was over. Oil was in the ground, and optimism laced the air. Happy days were here again.

"Tank farm" in Mexia oil field, 1924. Claude Brown at right.

CHAPTER FOUR

Early Oil Field Days

Three great waves of oil exploration have swept over Texas. The first wave, sparked by the Ranger strike of 1917, lasted until the early thirties. The second period spanned mid-1930s to the end of World War II. The third wave began in the late forties.

After World War I, the use of automobiles expanded and demand for gasoline rose rapidly. From 1918 to 1920, the price of crude oil in the United States climbed fifty percent. Price increases added to the perceived possibility of a decreasing supply, and the stampede to find oil was on.

As the rip-roaring decade of the 1920s opened, the price was a firm three dollars a barrel — enough to attract the adventurous and aggressive from around the world.

Claude Brown graduated from Ballinger High School in 1922 with only one question on his mind: whether to go to Texas A&M or to the University of Texas in the fall.

When his great-uncle, J. K. Hughes, offered Claude a job for the summer in the Mexia fields, Claude jumped at the chance to make money for college. Robust and husky at 5' 7, strong from farm labor, he could perform the hard work the oil fields demanded. On May 23 he boarded a train for Mexia, in the blacklands between the Brazos and Trinity rivers.

Mexia, a rich field discovered in 1920, had its day in the sun just as Claude Brown was breaking into the oil business. The town of 2,500 people went to 30,000 virtually overnight.

At its peak Mexia displayed all the features of the boomtowns

Workers in Mexia oil field in 1924. Claude Brown is third from right, a twenty-year-old learning the oil business.

Mexia oil field, 1924. Claude Brown at left.

Not all wells are winners. This twisted pile of burned-out rubble was payoff on a well drilled in Pecos County in the 1950s by Brown & Thorp Drilling Company.

A monstrous oil field fire killed fourteen men at Mexia in 1924. Claude Brown began as a gauger in this field after the fire was extinguished.

of its day. Gamblers, bootleggers, con men, adventurers, and ladies for rent mingled with the land men, scouts, drillers, pumpers, roughnecks, and roustabouts who combed the cotton patches and cane brakes of East Texas looking for their pot of gold. Martial law was enforced for two years.

Drilling centered northwest of town. Clanking, thumping cable-tool rigs gouged at the soft blackland soil. Makeshift dirt roads connected the field to homes and stores in town. Hordes of vehicles drawn by mules or horses competed with new and popular "Tin Lizzies" for a view of the derricks. After a moderate rain the roads became puddles; after a heavy rain they turned into small lakes of slippery, sticky black mud.

Claude began work as a roustabout on the Ellis lease operated by J. K. Hughes Oil Company. Hughes was the brother of Wilson Hughes, the grandfather from whom Claude Wilson Brown received his middle name.

The word "roustabout" is used in several trades. The roustabout "totes the bar and lifts the bale" on which society runs. He is the worker who sets up the tent when the circus comes to town. The roustabout performs unskilled labor on the lowest rung of the oil industry's ladder.

For the rest of his life, Claude Brown would refer to himself as "a roustabout from McCamey." He took pride in the label; he considered it the designation of an honest man who went into the marketplace and gave value for value: a day's work for a day's pay.

Living accommodations for a tenderfoot roustabout on the Hughes lease included a cot in the bunkhouse and meals at a boardinghouse. Two of Claude's bunkhouse buddies, Ben Crowder and John Turner, became his lifelong friends. Crowder and Turner, mature and experienced at twenty-two compared to the seventeen-year-old greenhorn, showed Claude the ropes of oil field life.

Claude learned his trade on the standard cable-tool rig of the twenties. The rig was eighty-two feet high, built of heavy lumber that housed the drilling machinery. Cable-tool drilling is accomplished by using the basic principle of the seesaw. The fulcrum is a sturdy, upright timber that stands six to eight feet high. A longer pole, known in the oil fields as the "Samson post," is balanced on the fulcrum so that one end fits exactly over the hole being dug. The other end is attached to the driving mechanism, which in the 1920s was usually a boiler-powered steam engine.

Drilling was an art as much as a science. The driller used equipment evolved from primitive tools. The skilled driller developed a "feel" for the way in which the drilling bit chewed into the earth. Like the cowboy and the riverboat pilot, the driller acquired an individualistic style that was admired in the West.

By tightening and loosening the lines connecting the drill bit to other parts of the machinery, the driller could get an idea of what kind of formation the bit was penetrating and could adjust the drilling pace. The rhythmic *ka-thump, ka-thump, ka-thump-thump* of the walking beams guided the driller in his effort to probe the earth for oil.

Starting at the lowest point, Brown worked to learn the techniques of "making hole." Like thousands of others who went to the oil fields to "take a look," he spent the rest of his life in the complex and challenging business of finding and producing oil.

"I was going to college in the fall. But when the time came, I thought I was making so much money that I didn't need an education," Brown laughed. "Working twelve to fifteen hours a day for seventy-five cents to a dollar a day on the farm . . . going from that to fifty cents an hour for nine hours a day looked like a million to me. So I stayed on the job, making twenty-seven dollars a week."

In July 1925 Claude received a promotion and transfer to Cross Plains as head of drilling and production. Given a choice of Smackover, Arkansas, or Cross Plains, he chose the Texas location.

J. K. Hughes Oil Company drilled fifty wells in the Cross Plains area. They were shallow wells, averaging 1,500 feet, most of them good producers.

In Cross Plains Claude met and courted Christine Grace McGowan, daughter of a local merchant.

"We were drilling there in town on her father's lot. I thought we would make a well and Christine would be rich. She thought I was a well-fixed oil man — so we were both fooled!"

Claude and Christine married in the Cross Plains Methodist Church February 20, 1926: a lively, unliberated young woman and her man of many wiles. Hard times and heartbreak would come later; so would the five-carat diamond ring. Claude made the living; Christine made the living worthwhile.

For the next sixty-one years, until Christine's death, the sky was the limit.

Society shifted into high gear in the twenties, its traditional norms and values eerily distorted. Prohibition, jazz, gangsters, speakeasies, and stocks on margin caught the public imagination. Cynical, materialistic, rather sad, the decade was an awkward period between wars. America seemed to have spent its idealism winning the war. The war to end wars had ended, but it was difficult to determine exactly what had been won. Europe, historic source of stability in the Western world, had collapsed into economic and social disorder.

"The Allies floated to victory on a wave of oil," said Viscount Curzon after the 1918 armistice. For the next ten years, America apparently intended to float its way to prosperity on the same sea.

By 1928 Texas, with a quarter billion barrels, led all states in oil production.

The nation's demand for fuel increased almost exponentially every decade. So hungry was the American economy for oil that wildcatters finally entered a most unpromising region: the Permian Basin.

CHAPTER FIVE

Depression Years

The Great Depression struck Claude Brown just as it did the rest of the world — as a sudden and unexpected cataclysm.

In October 1929 Brown was gaining speed as a drilling contractor in a flourishing business. Six months later he huddled in a dilapidated farmhouse two miles from Coleman, Texas. He was no longer closing in on the American dream. He was, instead, trying to figure out where the next meal could be found.

Three families of refugees from the economic catastrophe occupied the farmhouse: Claude and his bride Christine, and Claude's brothers, Tom and Homer, and their families.

"The Depression got us." This pithy statement described the down-and-out days of the early thirties. America had experienced depressions in 1837, 1873 and 1893, but the crisis beginning in October 1929 is the only depression with a capital "D."

Starting as a teenage roustabout, Brown had worked his way to the position of drilling and production superintendent in the Cross Plains area for the J. K. Hughes Oil Company. J. K. Hughes had become a wealthy man during the oil booms of the twenties in the Southwest. He had started from scratch, an old and honorable tradition in the oil patch, and had built a shoe-string operation into a big and profitable firm. He operated a string of fourteen cable-tool rigs and had accumulated some production. He sold the J. K. Hughes Oil Company in 1928.

When the Hughes firm was sold, Claude Brown was working in Cross Plains with his friend from Mexia days, Ben Crowder, as

23

his production superintendent. Each man had saved a little money. Claude and Ben pooled their resources, bought a rig, and went into business on their own. Their venture was successful.

Brown had mastered the craft of drilling by working in the new fields then being developed in East Texas—Currie, Wortham, Corsicana, and others. He learned the production side of the business; learned how to deal with the oil after it has been brought up out of the ground, and how to get it to market.

A year later Crowder left the partnership to return to East Texas and operate a rotary rig. In what was then a common mishap, the drill pipe stuck and literally pulled the rig into the hole, killing Crowder.

Claude Brown moved his drilling business from Cross Plains to Coleman, located about halfway between Cross Plains and Ballinger. There he contracted to drill wells in the fields nearby: Strawn, Abilene, and other parts of West Central Texas.

Prospects looked good for the young man from Ballinger nearing his twenty-fifth birthday, absorbed in the bold business of finding and producing oil. Claude Brown, optimistic by nature, had an outlook that mirrored the national attitude toward business: he was confident that the future would be bright, the sun would shine forever.

Optimism was the official party line from the Hoover White House, and most of the nation agreed. Had not prices on the New York Stock Exchange doubled between early 1928 and September 1929? The fact that trading was done principally on borrowed money—a "margin" of ten percent in most stock purchases—did not lessen the country's pervasive optimism.

"Everybody ought to be rich," advised industrialist John J. Raskob, and there were few dissenters. Such euphoria was a classic example of what the English historian Charles Mackay had labeled in 1841 *The Madness of Crowds*.

People believe what they want to believe, and crowds tend to go too far. "Men, it has been well said, think in herds," observed Mackay. "It will be seen that they go mad in herds, while they only recover their senses slowly and one by one."

The bubble burst on Thursday, October 24, 1929, on the floor of the New York Stock Exchange.

Accounts of the Great Depression, its causes, effects and after-the-fact advice, fill our libraries. Its causes are still debated; its

effects were immediate and devastating. A multi-year deflation-
ary spiral tore at the fabric of American society as nothing else
has done, before or since. Jobs, homes, careers, farms, factories,
stores, and lives were sucked into its great black hole.

Wall Street's collapse affected oil immediately. In less than
three months, crude oil prices fell drastically. Low prices fed on
themselves until they went below the cost of production — much
less the cost of drilling new exploratory wells.

Drilling activity ceased almost entirely. The price of crude
oil, never stable, began a long slide that ended at ten cents a
barrel two years later.

It cost from seventy-four cents to one dollar to produce one
barrel of crude oil. Sinking prices left drilling operations at a
standstill. The demand for gasoline continued to increase; the
world had an insatiable appetite for automobiles. But the supply
side of the supply-demand equation was unpredictable. Every
discovery of a large field brought a glut and lower prices, at least
temporarily.

Price volatility, always a hazard in the petroleum business,
became chaotic during the early thirties. Stories still circulate of
Permian Basin producers who were forced, by unusual selling
agreements, to pay a purchaser to take crude oil.

One scenario goes as follows. The posted price is sixty cents
per barrel and prices are fluctuating in a range of fifty to seventy-
five cents. A small producer, desperate to create cash flow, agrees
with a buyer to sell at a price "at thirty-five cents below the posted
price, whatever it may be." A deal is made, and oil is delivered at
a beginning price of twenty-five cents a barrel. The posted price
plummets to twenty-nine cents a barrel. On each barrel of crude
under this contract, the buyer hauls the oil away, being paid six
cents a barrel. The story sounds incredible; those were incredible
times.

From the first super-boom at Spindletop, where temporary
overproduction forced prices as low as three cents a barrel, the
pattern of feast-or-famine was firmly established. As the global
economy shrank in the thirties, demand for oil plummeted. Work
for drilling crews was almost nonexistent by mid-1930.

Brown tried to keep his rig going in the scattered fields around
Coleman, but the economic situation grew worse. Rapidly and
inexorably, the life blood of available drilling funds — money to
find new oil — evaporated.

By June 1930 Brown had lost all his business and personal assets. His cable-tool rig, his car, his savings account, and any assets he could sell—all vanished in the bottomless depths of the Depression.

The next five years were a time of testing and survival, a scrambling, hand-to-mouth existence. Remembering those years, Brown later appreciated their redeeming features.

"It was hard, but we seemed to enjoy it. We were all in the same boat at that time," he recalled. "From 1930 until I came to McCamey in 1935, looking back on it now, it was not too serious a time. We all enjoyed each other. Neighbors were more willing to share with each other."

Family life was sweet. "We cut our own hair, with our wives helping. We did not go to movies. We had no telephone. If we had money to make a call, we would go into town and make it from a pay phone. It cost a nickel for a local call."

Two nickels bought a loaf of bread. Gasoline sold for fifteen cents a gallon. Beefsteak cost twenty-five cents a pound.

Entertainment consisted mostly of conversation. "We made our own entertainment by just talking, trying to figure out what would be the next move we could make."

The unemployed oil field workers gathered daily in the Culver Hotel in Coleman. In a group of five or ten, one man would occasionally have a spare nickel to buy a *Fort Worth Star-Telegram*. The newspaper would be passed around among members of the group until everyone had seen it. Newspapers were scanned closely for news of any oil developments or related economic news.

Claude Brown provided for his family by landing a few days' work occasionally. Times got worse for oil field workers in West Texas with the discovery of the vast East Texas oil deposits.

On October 3, 1930, Daisy Bradford No. 3 blew in on a sandyland Rusk County farm. It opened the biggest oil field ever seen in the United States. Overproduction immediately sent the price of crude oil into the industry's now famous swan dive. Lower prices, far below the cost of production, further inhibited drilling activity in other areas of the state.

In order to survive, Claude Brown was forced to develop some source of income other than cable-tool drilling. Two skills enabled him to eke out a living: hunting and trading.

The three Brown families sharing a farmhouse had a milk

cow, a garden, and a few chickens. This provender supplied milk, eggs and vegetables, but it put no meat on the table. In the American tradition of living off the land, Brown used his .22-caliber rifle and became expert at hunting jackrabbits.

No individual born after 1935 has had any direct exposure to the Depression or to the hardships endured by the average American family in that decade. The idea of hunting for any reason except sport is foreign to most Americans. It was not so during the thirties. The meat of a jackrabbit is much like chicken. Served in the midst of a diet of beans, a piece of fried rabbit tasted delicious.

Boys growing up in Texas learned how to use a gun. After all, rural areas in Texas were not far removed from the frontier. Thousands of men hunted for their food in the thirties, and were thankful to have the opportunity.

Claude's distant cousin, a teenager on a poverty-stricken cotton farm in North Texas, was encouraged by his father to save ammunition when he hunted small game. A .22-caliber long cartridge cost forty-one cents per hundred in the Sears Roebuck catalog; a good hunter could not afford to waste such high-priced ammunition.

The kid learned to shoot straight, to save on ammunition. He then went on to become America's most-decorated hero of World War II, an infantryman from Farmersville, Texas, named Audie Murphy.

Claude's fortunes got so low that he could not always afford ammunition. In that case, he would supply the gun and the shooting eye, find an "investor" who could put up the ammunition, and hunt rabbits on the halves. One had to be an expert marksman to make such a deal.

The long, deep paralysis appeared to have no end. Outgoing President Herbert Hoover, discouraged about the "final triumph over poverty" he had envisioned for America, voiced the spirit of the times: "We are at the end of our string. There is nothing more we can do."

The Depression traumatized writers and artists. Economic chaos bred political dissension. Radical social approaches were brewed around the globe: communism in Russia, fascism in Spain and Italy, the Nazi Party in Germany. Angst spread across America as well. The breakdown of society in the thirties was creating the ideological and moral vacuums that eventually ignited World War II.

The twenties and early thirties produced a Golden Age of ideological exotica. Books by the dozen appeared on the Great Depression. Self-styled thinkers wrote, spoke, and launched movements. Through the alphabet, from A to Z, reformers devised a cause for every letter. New cures and formulas appeared daily.

While theorists expounded on the crisis, the Depression functioned with a life of its own. Practical people lived their lives one day at a time and pulled through. In the history of the long Texas frontier, the man who learned and adapted was the man who survived. Chance had little to do with it.

Claude, by this time, had reached back into his ancestral gene pool and connected with a long-forgotten pioneer trader who practiced the art of the possible.

"There was no money," he said. "We did a lot of barter."

At the bottom of the Depression, October 15, 1931, Claude and Christine received the gift of their lifetime: their only child, a daughter, was born. They named her Claudyne.

This birth at the farm home of Christine's parents brought immense joy as well as another crisis: a doctor's bill for eighty-five dollars. The bill was a bit expensive, Claude admitted, but it did include six months of prenatal care as well as the delivery.

Claude learned by necessity to trade in used oil field equipment. He heard there was a cotton gin at Valera, in Coleman County, that needed oil for fuel. He went to the gin and negotiated a price of seventy-five cents per barrel, delivered. He then scoured the local area for the best price to buy, and found an oil dealer in Cross Plains who would sell at twenty-five cents a barrel. He bought oil in Cross Plains and sold it to the Valera gin thirty-five miles away. The profit paid the medical bill for Claudyne's delivery.

Claude decided that trading was just about the only way he could provide for his family.

One staple item in drilling a well is the casing pipe, the sheath of metal protecting the hole in the earth from being filled in with debris from the drilling operation. Such pipe usually changed hands at one to two dollars a foot. Claude was able, on one occasion, to make a deal for standard size eight and one-quarter-inch casing at twenty cents per foot, and for ten and three-quarter-inch pipe for fifty cents a foot.

Few Americans had foreseen the economic collapse. In the spring of 1929 a brainy young bond salesman, walking the canyons of Wall Street, grew alarmed at the speculation he saw in the financial world. On sheer intuition he sold his securities, shut down his successful firm, advised his clients to do the same, and retired to Florida to wait out the situation.

Few individuals were as perceptive as Charles Merrill. The majority of Americans were content to believe the joy ride would go on and on.

Survival for Claude, Christine and Claudyne meant living a hand-to-mouth existence. An occasional few days' work might turn up for a strong, experienced oil field hand. A trade might be worked out on a few feet of pipe or some hand tools used on a drilling rig. But trades were few and far between.

Similar episodes of "make-do, or do without" were commonplace. A friend of Claude's had prospered by 1929 and, like many Texans before and since, had bought himself a ranch. He found 1,800 acres in Hamilton County, paid for it, and stocked it with ewes at six dollars a head. When he moved onto the ranch Thanksgiving Day, 1931, the ewes could have been bought for a dollar and fifty cents per head.

Oil companies that were glamour stocks of the 1920s suffered in the Wall Street crash along with other industries. Shares of the major companies had been favorite investments of oil field people.

Full production became only a memory. One car was produced in 1932 for every three produced in 1929. Retail food prices fell by forty percent. It was more difficult to come up with sixty cents, however, than to raise a dollar in 1929. Four million families had gone on relief with an average family benefit of fifteen dollars per month. Unemployment figures could not be relied upon, but one in four is a figure often used.

Across the nation — indeed, around the world — spirits sank, money vanished, barter developed. New ways of thought tempted the working man in an effort to replace the old certainties that seemed lost. Scientific discoveries posed new human problems, for which there seemed to be no acceptable answers. The world went on a binge of hypothesizing a crisis of the mind, which saw new ideologies create the destructive patterns of the twentieth century. The world, the United States, and the state of Texas sank into a baleful blue funk.

A more immediate problem than global economic theory occupied Claude — that of finding food and shelter for himself, his wife, and his daughter. He laughed about his experience in trying to get on relief.

"The city of Cross Plains was in the process of laying new water and sewer lines, under the Public Works Administration. I tried to get a job with them and they said, 'NO.' I even told them I was a Democrat, but they still said, 'NO, you are in the oil business.'"

The PWA was a part of the National Recovery Act created by the administration of Franklin D. Roosevelt. Its aim was to prime the pump; to help business by raising purchasing power.

Dave Duncan, a short red-haired ex-sailor, was a neighbor of the Browns in Cross Plains. Duncan owned a cable-tool drilling rig. Brown had met Duncan when he was drilling for J. K. Hughes; Duncan at the time was drilling in Howard County, west of Cross Plains.

Early in 1935 Claude Brown hit bottom economically. He and Christine and three-year-old Claudyne moved in with Christine's parents. Scratching for work to pay his bills, Claude made a far-reaching phone call:

> I was stranded in early 1935 at the McGowans in Cross Plains. I was very depressed, but I figured that with my experience and knowledge of the oil business I could somehow make a comeback if I only had a chance. I had lost my rig, my car, and I was flat broke. Even turned down by the Public Works Administration for a job laying water lines.
>
> In desperation I called my friend Dave Duncan and told him my problem. He said, "I am starting a well for Conoco at Bakersfield, in Upton County; go to McCamey and report to my tool pusher, Dee Breeding."
>
> I had worked with Dee Breeding in Mexia in 1922 and had given him contracts to drill wells in Brown County for J. K. Hughes Oil Company when I was their superintendent.
>
> My next problem was to get to McCamey with no car and no money. I found this old Oldsmobile that my friend said he would sell for sixty-five dollars cash. I tried at the bank for a loan; the bank said, "No" (just like the PWA).
>
> I finally talked my friend into letting me take the car and pay him for it after the first pay day.

I filled the tank with drip gasoline — that's a low-octane, high volatility poor man's fuel — and went by Brownwood to see a man who owed me money for drilling a well. He said, "Brown, I am struggling for beans myself."

I got to Ballinger and spent the night with my mother and dad. Mother let me have five dollars to buy gasoline; it was about fifteen cents a gallon. I had to stop on the road and patch flat tires all the way from San Angelo to McCamey.

It was an awful hot August day. The car would vapor lock; I would have to take the gasoline line loose and blow it out with my mouth to get the gasoline back into the carburetor.

Finally I got to McCamey. I had never been farther west than San Angelo. Not all the roads were paved at that time. I probably drove only twenty to thirty miles per hour on account of my papershell tires.

Claude's associate, Dave Duncan, had a similar experience. Both drillers—young in years but old in experience—were rescued by the revival of certain oil fields in West Texas. The process of acidizing had stirred new interest in old oil wells. New fields were discovered. Acidizing is the injection of chemicals, such as hydrochloric acid, into wells to clean out and dissolve pores in oil-bearing formations. This process stimulates oil production.

Oil fields around McCamey have had several revivals since the first field in 1925. Acidizing brought a new boom in the mid-thirties. The demands of World War II and the Cold War brought another boom, and the OPEC-triggered price explosion of the 1980s again increased the demand for wells, including smaller-producing ones.

"I was sitting around the hotel with no money whatsoever," said Dave Duncan, "and a fellow came along one day and wanted me to go out to McCamey with him and look the country over. I went with him. It began to look like West Texas was going to come back in the oil business. I got interested in going out there.

"I made a deal with a party to drill a wildcat well on the McKinsey ranch, which is better known as the Girvin Field up in Pecos County, about seventeen miles southwest of Pecos. I moved my rig down there from Big Spring and put this well down."

Dave Duncan hired Claude Brown for a dollar an hour.

CHAPTER SIX

Reaching McCamey

Together they had reached McCamey, Odysseus and his ship, moving west over the unseen sea of oil beneath them. The traveler climbed out of his shuddering Oldsmobile and wiped caliche dust from his face and hands.

McCamey, at the western edge of the Edwards Plateau, is the last town east of the Pecos River, where wood and water run out. Pecos country is legendary for buried treasure. Franciscan friars, outlaws robbing the U. S. Army payroll, and Texas mercenaries riding for the Mexican emperor Maximilian are all believed to have hidden chests of gold coins and bullion in the caves of Pecos country.

Claude Brown came into McCamey in search of another form of riches. He was not, in truth, looking for a place to spend the rest of his life. On that August day McCamey was just another oil field town, thrown together in the quickest, cheapest manner possible.

Who would have believed that the weary pilgrim pulling into the Clark Hotel would become Mr. McCamey?

Claude Wilson Brown had less than a dollar in his pocket, only the few coins left from the five-dollar bill his mother had loaned him to buy gasoline.

He owed for the car. He owed for the gasoline that got him to McCamey. He needed a bath and a square meal, and he needed to locate a man named Dee Breeding.

Brown had one thing in his favor: he carried the poor man's

passport on which to travel during the thirties. He had a job, the ultimate credential for doing business in the Depression.

Mr. Clark preferred to have a hotel room occupied by a driller with an IOU rather than have an empty room. Credit until payday? Sure, Mr. Brown, and you can eat in the dining room. When he did draw a paycheck a month later, it was paid not in currency but in coupon books issued by the Continental Oil Company.

The oil industry had lived in a state of semi-crisis since the East Texas field was opened. Overproduction and chaotic pricing kept the industry off balance. Oil men carried around a mental magic number: one dollar a barrel. Oil would get to that price and stay there several weeks, but price fragility and volatility were the oil man's constant adversaries in the marketplace.

Corporations, like individuals, at times ran short of cash. Companies then resorted to the use of scrip in the form of coupon books, such as those used by Conoco. Merchants accepted the coupons and redeemed them later for currency.

Old-timers say that McCamey was operating mostly on scrip in the mid-thirties.

Brown located Dee Breeding and worked as his driller on the Bakersfield well. It was a dry hole. He was still living in the Clark Hotel, saving money to move Christine and Claudyne to McCamey.

The reunion almost did not take place. After the Conoco dry hole, a second well was drilled on the same lease west of McCamey near a landmark known as Squaw Teat Mountain. Brown, working on this crew as a tool pusher, had a close call with poisonous gas.

On a cable-tool rig, a device known as the bailer is dropped into the hole every few feet. The bailer lifts up broken clods of earth. Brown tied the twenty-five-foot marker used to indicate the new depth, but he did not step back quickly enough. He later described what happened:

> When I stepped back to hang up my marker, the whole world began to swing around and I passed out.
>
> About thirty minutes later the driller had dragged me out to the end of the walk from the rig floor. He said he had about given up on me and was going down to the store and post office at Bakersfield and call an ambulance to come and get me.
>
> He had me lying on my stomach with his arm under me,

rolling my stomach as hard as he could. I heard from a far distance someone say, "Brown, Brown, Brown . . ." It finally came a little closer. I said, "Where am I?"

"You've been gassed," the driller said. "I've been working on you for thirty minutes. I was ready to give up when I heard your voice."

At that moment I began to vomit. The driller brought me into McCamey to see a doctor.

Fossil fuels such as oil do not come out of the earth clean and ready for use. In their natural state they contain impurities, the most dangerous one being sulphur. Certain oil fields of West Texas are notorious for their sulphur content. Brown had inhaled poisonous sulphur gas.

He returned to work on the rig a week later.

Pecos country is immense, brooding, unforgiving country, a part of the Chihuahuan Desert, with dry rocky mountains and jagged gashes in the earth. Comanche war parties swept over its greasewood plains to plunder settlements in Chihuahua and Durango. Gold prospectors drove wagons through its desert to California. Trail bosses herded cattle across the Pecos to northern markets, their thirsty livestock at times crazed into stampeding when they smelled the fatally alkaline Pecos River. (Animal skulls bleaching in the sun inspired the name Horsehead Crossing.)

Claude Brown drove into McCamey on August 4, 1935.

Was it hot?

"It was hot as baked hell." Men who lived in McCamey used this simile of choice when they said hello.

Claude Brown, broke and in debt, rolled down the parched road on just that kind of day. He could remember vividly what he saw:

Shotgun shacks on the outskirts of town, close to the T&P Tavern. (These three-room houses were so named because, theoretically, one could fire a shotgun from front door to back door without damaging anything.)

A "city limit" sign on a dust-coated piece of one-by-four lumber just before Main Street, the narrowest street in town.

Three or four blocks of businesses, beginning with the Humble Oil service station.

On the south side of Main Street, the Buick-Chevrolet dealer;

on the north side, the Ford dealer. Fisher's drug store and a variety store; a hardware store and funeral home. The biggest building in town was the two-story Bender Hotel. Next door stood Bender Dry Goods.

Bank, barber shop, and dress shop. Echo Drug, Bill Baugh's newsstand, Brownie's parlor, grocery store, and the two-story frame McCamey Hotel. Queen Theater, Western Union office, Justice of the Peace. A store converted to a church. More shanties out on Highway 67 leading to Fort Stockton, forty-six miles into the western sun.

McCamey was eight years old as an incorporated municipality in 1935. Six or eight thousand souls lived within its limits. A procession of adventurous individuals had walked the board sidewalks on Main Street since George McCamey's discovery well in 1925.

George B. McCamey and a handful of his fellow wildcatters had proved, in the twenties, that there was oil in commercial amounts beneath the West Texas plains. During the Depression, drilling stopped almost entirely. Through the early thirties the posted price (the official selling price per barrel of crude oil) hovered around twenty-five cents. At times it sold even lower; East Texas oil was hitting the market at ten to fifteen cents a barrel. Bankrupt banks, ruined retailers, abandoned mortgages, and millions of unemployed men and women littered the economic landscape – and made a dollar an hour look good to a tapped-out driller.

McCamey's Main Street in 1935 was narrow and dusty. Two cars traveling in opposite directions barely had room to pass. The Bender Hotel was the busiest place in town. Upton County's sheriff worked out of Rankin, the county seat eighteen miles away. Overall, the town wore the unmistakable "morning after" look of a boomtown after the boom: used up, worn out, waiting for a break.

Brown later estimated that half a million individuals passed through McCamey during the half century after the 1925 discovery. "You're not a real Permian Basin resident until you've been through McCamey" became a common expression. (Meaning: until you've worked there, or gone there on business.)

Population in the twenties and thirties, except for a corporal's guard of natives, could be labeled mostly boomers. Restless by nature, they had gained mobility (courtesy of Henry Ford) and they intended to see the action.

History thrives on its cutting edge. Oil fields such as McCamey —or Borger or Ranger or Smackover or a dozen others—drew the energetic, capable, and adventurous individual. There was no demand for the weak, the fearful, or the slow-witted at the driller's post on a cable-tool rig platform.

For cosmopolitanism, nothing surpasses an oil town during a boom. Frenchman and Pennsylvanian, Yankee and Southerner, Scot and Hebrew, European and Latin, dreamer and doer, scholar and scoundrel, rough and gentle: all types swarm to a place like McCamey. Most of them move on.

McCamey pioneer Anna Wolf in 1970 summarized the ups and downs of a typical oil field town:

> Most people, when they came in they thought they would only be here a month or so. If you are that temporary, you are not going to put much money in a house. When people once decided they were going to be here longer, they began to build better houses.
>
> We had two jewelry stores (I can't recall their names), but when they made their money they sold out and left. Then after the Humble Oil Company lost its refinery (it caught fire), the town began to go down. About 1936 or 1937 it picked up again. All during the war the town was good. It went downhill again in the early 1950s.[1]

Mrs. Wolf saw all three Permian Basin booms from a strategic viewpoint. A favorite pastime in czarist Russia was the occasional pogrom. William Wolf, a citizen of Odessa, Russia, cast a critical eye upon his country and decided to excuse himself from duty as a martyr. He set out for America.

Willie Wolf wound up in Ranger. After that boom, he went to McCamey in 1927. Wolf dealt in used oil field equipment through McCamey's good times and bad.

Claude Brown came on stage at the end of the first phase. When McCamey began its second boom, he was in position to recoup his fortunes and go on to become "Mr. McCamey."

CHAPTER SEVEN

Second Boom

Oil men are nomads, largely by instinct, often by necessity.

Families that followed the booms were forced to adopt a nomadic lifestyle. Since Mother Nature had seen fit to distribute most of the earth's supply of hydrocarbons in out-of-the-way places, those who followed the trade learned to travel. Families of oil field workers adjusted to a distinctive way of life: jobs were sought in new and active fields, the wage earner went anywhere a job could be found, and the family came later. This standard procedure was followed by Claude, Christine, and Claudyne Brown.

Claude worked on the drilling rig at Bakersfield, lived at the Clark Hotel, and saved pennies to bring his wife and daughter to join him. Two months later the three moved into their first McCamey "home," a one-room apartment.

Claude's toughest daily chore was transportation to and from Bakersfield well, twenty miles west of town. He worked the evening tour from 4:00 p.m. to midnight—a trip his Oldsmobile could not make without extra water. Around 3:00 every afternoon, Claude would fill a five-gallon can with water and stow it in the car. Once he had driven a few miles down the road, the radiator would begin to boil.

A windmill stood at Girvin, a crossroads between McCamey and Bakersfield. Twice each day, en route to and from his tour of duty, Claude would stop at the windmill to fill up his radiator and his five-gallon spare water can.

The Girvin windmill later became Brown's good luck symbol.

"I am afraid to get too far away to drill a well," he told his friends. "We discovered three fields nearly within a stone's throw of that old windmill. It will always have a special place in my heart."

Claude Brown had landed in one of the few spots in the United States that offered economic opportunity. McCamey's first production was recorded in 1925; serious amounts began to appear the following year. Tents and shacks mushroomed on the prairie. The lusty young city was, however, wiped out during the Depression. It was beginning to make a comeback when Brown arrived.

McCamey proved to be a good place for a trader. Working for Duncan on the evening tours, he became a daytime moonlighter dealing in oil field materials. Old friends at Ranger, Coleman, and Mexia became his source of supply.

After a year of two-shift activity, Brown quit Duncan and went out on his own. A year later he opened Brown Pipe and Supply Company. He bought a supply store in Grandfalls, a tiny oil town in Ward County. Three years later he owned six stores located in active drilling areas of the Permian Basin, in West Texas and New Mexico.

From dealing in oil field supplies, he expanded into drilling and production. Years later Brown diversified further into banking, car dealerships, and real estate. Various businesses stemmed from his moonlighting from a cable-tool driller's job in 1935.

Several factors contributed to Brown's string of business successes. First, his arrival in McCamey was fortuitously timed to participate in the city's second boom. Second, the nation was beginning to pick itself up off the floor economically, as the stimulative measures of Franklin D. Roosevelt's New Deal programs began to kick in. The late 1930s also saw the build-up of industry leading into World War II.

In a sense Claude Brown's business career after August 4, 1935, could be compared to an investor who happened to pick the low day of a long bear market to buy his first share of stock. The "timing is everything" school of thought will make this interpretation.

There is another explanation. Brown had paid his dues for fourteen years; he knew the business. He was an energetic and unyielding optimist. He was also eaten up with the work ethic, handed down to him by Scotch-Irish ancestors who considered work something to enjoy rather than to avoid.

A West Texan who knew C. W. Brown forty-seven years had this to say: "In my judgment, luck had little to do with C. W. Brown's success in any field of endeavor. Success has come to him because he was willing to work longer, harder and more diligently than his competitors."

Jim Langdon, chairman of the Texas Railroad Commission, made that statement. He met Brown in January 1946, when he drove into snow-covered McCamey looking for a place to settle down and raise a family.

"Claude applied the rules of hard work in everything he has undertaken, whether as a member of the church, as mayor of McCamey, or as a private citizen," said Langdon.

His lawyer knew Brown well; the older man gave Langdon his first legal business in 1946, and Langdon served as Brown's attorney for eight years.

Claude, Christine, and Claudyne lived in their tiny apartment for two years. In his spare time, Claude made deals with old friends in Central Texas for second-hand equipment he could sell in the Permian Basin. He liked trading and would consider anything.

Then he ran across an unusual opportunity: the chance to buy a service station. An old Continental Oil Company station on Highway 67, the main east-west route through town, was for sale.

Entrepreneur Brown knew by that time what he wanted to do. He had landed in an oil field that had gone through a spectacular boom, collapsed, dragged along the bottom several years, and now maybe—a mighty big maybe—looked as if it had the seeds of renewal. Claude Brown, at thirty-three, had seen both sides of the boom-and-bust picture in the oil industry. Another boom was in the making in West Texas, he decided, and he wanted in.

Brown bought the old station and converted the rear of the building into a small but snug apartment. On the front he hung a sign: C. W. Brown Pipe and Supply Company.

From that modest roadside enterprise came a flourishing drilling company, several hundred oil wells, several multi-million-dollar oil deals, a pipeline, bank, car dealership, and a sprawling collection of real estate in McCamey, Fort Worth, and Beaumont.

One man's boarded-up economic failure proved to be another man's opportunity. When his opportunity appeared, C. W. Brown was ready.

The first McCamey boom was like a West Texas sandstorm: sudden, random, violent and brief, leaving in its wake a stunned and empty stillness.

Baker No. 1, the project of wildcatter George B. McCamey, blew in among the creosote bushes of Upton County in 1925. By the end of the year the boom was in high gear. It lasted until 1929-30, derailed by two events: the Great Depression and the "black giant" of the great East Texas oil field. Shallower wells in East Texas meant easier and less expensive drilling. Frequent gushers in the East Texas field decimated the West Texas oil industry, including production in McCamey.

Oil wells of Upton, Crane, Crockett, and Pecos counties, surrounding McCamey, were relatively shallow; the Baker discovery hit pay at 2,193 feet. Several pay zones were missed in the rush.

Brown became interested in abandoned wells. He figured that under certain conditions some wells could be made profitable.

One type of well that offered opportunity, he calculated, was the well that had been drilled too deep and had penetrated a water-bearing formation. This situation permitted water encroachment and watered out the oil. Previous operators had produced the wells as long as they showed a profit, then abandoned them.

Within a sixty-mile radius of McCamey lay hundreds of abandoned wells. Some had been properly shut down and abandoned; some had not.

Brown began an intensive study of well logs. He searched continually for any log he could find. Gradually he was able to put together a mental picture of oil-bearing formations below the alkaline surface. He would then make an offer, sometimes sight unseen, on any abandoned property he could find.

One way to make a producer from a shut-down well was simply to drill deeper. It was possible in some cases to set new pipe, go deeper, and frequently come up with new, fresh production. Some old wells would yield new production "up hole," where the original drilling had passed through a potential zone of production without a completion.

Wells around McCamey averaged 2,200 to 2,400 feet in depth. A 600-foot elevation north of town, King's Mountain, had the effect of increasing the depth of some wells to 2,800 to 3,000 feet. Drilling costs in the 1930s were about two dollars and fifty cents per foot for cable-tool drilling. Most operators figured they could "put one on the pump" at that time for a total cost of about $20,000.

Another factor affecting the oil business was the technique of acidizing. The objective is larger underground pores, freer movement of oil, and better production. Acidizing played an increasingly important role in the Permian Basin after 1936.

Revival of interest in West Texas drilling, an improved overall economic picture, technological advances, and new ways of looking at old situations combined to form fertile ground for Brown's enterprising nature.

Traders need to borrow money to operate. Brown's ability to borrow was always a significant factor in his life. In 1935 he managed to borrow $435 from the Security State Bank in McCamey.

"Mark McWhorter, our banker, got out on a limb and loaned me my first money since the Depression days," he said. "He knew that acidizing had just come in."

A man born to trade, an oil man in the middle of one of the world's great oil fields, a businessman coming into the prime of his life concurrently with an economic recovery and the beginnings of a major expansion of the national economy — all these factors plus his own sanguine temperament made Brown a borrower of money. He figured at one time that he owed thirty-two Texas banks.

"Be bold!" he urged his wife years later, as she dressed for a bridge game. "Bid high! Don't be afraid!"

Once Brown had reestablished his credentials, he found his lifelong calling as a wheeler-dealer. Small trades at first; later he reached the seven-figure deal. His penchant for making deals was probably as great in selling scrap tubing for a few dollars, or swapping second-hand pipe for an abandoned oil well, as in the ambitious transactions that came later.

He sought advice and information from the independent oil operators. He liked to drink coffee and talk with drillers and tool pushers. He asked a lot of questions, and tried to stay on good terms with all sources.

"I considered that information just as valuable then as it would have been to have a geologist — and I generally did not have the money to do things like I would have liked to do," he said.

Dozens of operators, independents and majors alike, have since used the same techniques of reviving old wells.

Jim Langdon did not expect any business from Brown. "C. W. had been discounted to me as a prospective client because he simply never had any money," Langdon explained. "He only did business with people he could trade things with."

But good sense prevailed over street talk. Langdon and Brown made a deal the first time they met. At a 1967 dinner Langdon would declare, "I have never known a better man than Claude Wilson Brown."

Brown would extend the compliment to his bankers: "Without bankers you cannot go. In 1936, I borrowed the limit the McCamey bank would loan to one man, $1,500. Went to Rankin, $2,500, the limit to one man. Had a pipe deal that took $5,000 to handle: came to Midland and went to Mr. Ulmer, introduced myself, he loaned me the $5,000. At that time the combined deposits in both Midland banks were only three million. Mr. Ulmer and Mr. John Butler, First National Bank, are responsible for starting me on what success I have had. Lots of times I would buy $50,000 or $100,000 in material, give checks, then come to borrow the money; my bankers never said no. I will admit that I have always been able to borrow too easy and from too many banks. Money is easier to borrow than it is to pay back."

One banker commented on C. W.'s tendency to overextend himself: "C. W. is inclined to spread himself just a little thin at times and I ought to worry about him. But I don't worry, because C. W. is always more worried about what he owes the bank than I am. I won't begin worrying until C. W. stops."

CHAPTER EIGHT

The Great McCamey Rattlesnake Derby

Write it in stone: Boomtowns attract what the world calls "a character."

The special combination of flamboyance, gall, charisma, and hustling ability that goes into the making of a character — a *persona* that stands out in the conventional world like neon in the dark — thrived in the oil field booms. A genuine character enjoyed full diplomatic status. In some cases, where his contribution to society struck a certain responsive chord with other boomers, the character became a cherished figure.

Such a man was P. L. Brown of McCamey (no relation to Claude Brown).

P. L. (as he was known before his reincarnation as "Rattlesnake Brownie") owned and operated a store on McCamey's Main Street. He attracted customers to his store with a display of rattlesnakes, the widespread family of pit vipers spread across North America. These little monsters differ from other snakes by virtue of an interlocking series of horny rings at the end of the tail, which produces an ominous rattling sound when shaken; hence their name.

The city-bound person who has never heard a rattler may recall the fatal clicking in dozens of suspense movies. The ominous sound precedes the terror scene. An angry rattlesnake sounds deadly, even if it is not visible. Alfred Hitchcock used it, and Hitchock knew ominous and deadly.

Upton County has an abundant supply of rattlesnakes. The

area is particularly well-provided with the species *crotalus adamanteus*, better known as the diamondback rattler.

The diamondback is a very ugly customer. It has markings on its back in a diamond-shaped pattern, and a flat, mean head with wide jaws. It blends in with the desert background and is almost invisible unless it wants to be seen. The serpent is, for its size, one of the most dangerous creatures on earth.

Mr. P. L. Brown, merchant, decided in the early thirties to use *crotalus adamanteus* to perk up his advertising program. He put them in the window for the benefit of men and women passing by. He kept a box of the reptiles, complete with rattlers and fangs, on display inside the store.

Going on a rattlesnake hunt was a rite of passage for a teenager growing up in McCamey, and other parts of the Permian Basin, in that era. The method was simple and dangerous. The hunter would use a tough, slender pole (a used or broken cue stick from a poolroom was excellent for the purpose) and would attach a stout hook to one end of the pole. The hunter poked his home-made weapon into a cave, a hole in the rock, or under an outcrop. (The rock-strewn mesas around McCamey near Castle Gap provided excellent hunting grounds.) He moved the pole around until he felt resistance, like a fish biting, and pulled out his catch. A shorter pole with a stout noose attached was thrown around the snake's head and tightened — and a rattlesnake was captured! A new addition to the advertising display of P. L. Brown.

Brown advanced from being just another minor character in the back row into the pantheon of big-time promoters with the small brainstorm he had in March 1933.

McCamey was nearing its sixth birthday. The city needed something special to commemorate birthday number six in style. A rodeo? No, rodeos in Texas are a dime a dozen. A "jackrabbit roping contest" such as neighboring Odessa had promoted in the 1920s? The sophisticated Eastern press would never bite twice on that one! What could McCamey do that was exciting, dramatic, dangerous . . . and cheap?

The idea, like all the great ones, was simple. P. L. talked his fellow merchants into sponsoring what became known as "The Great McCamey Rattlesnake Derby."

The competition would be for rattlesnakes what the Kentucky Derby is for horses. First, an elimination from the field of all but the most qualified entrants. The contest would have rules, a specified course, a starter, timer, and judges to make sure there was no snaky cheating. A physician stood by for the benefit of the snake handlers, not the derby entrants.

In early March, civic-minded McCameyites raided snake dens until they hauled in some 200 reptiles.

For the great Rattlesnake Derby, the McCamey High School Badgers' football team made their football field available. This contribution saved the expense of building bleachers for the crowd.

"Trainers" and "jockeys" were picked to handle the fifty prime candidates. A racetrack was built, the only racetrack in known history designed and built for *crotalus adamanteus*.

In the middle of the field, with the center at the midpoint of the fifty-yard line, a circle of 100 feet in diameter was marked off. Around it a "fence" of oil field cable was strung on the ground.

This was the racetrack. The starting point was Rattlesnake Brownie's specially constructed starting box in the center. The finish line was at any point on the cable encircling the track. In the center of the 100-foot-wide ring was the "Brownie box." This device was a custom-made steel box, with collapsible walls and a metal floor electrically wired. The box was wide, shallow, and just large enough to hold fifty rattlesnakes measuring four to seven feet long. The fifty loathsome creatures were selected from the initial group of 200 for physique and speed.

If there is one distinguishing characteristic of oil field people, it is their willingness to speculate on an uncertain outcome. The Rattlesnake Derby promoters, catering to this propensity, added a bingo element to the event.

Around the perimeter of the circle, set six feet apart, stood a series of wooden pegs numbered from one to fifty. Chances sold on each peg at five dollars. The sweepstakes purse of $250 would go to the winner.

Thus it was that on a sunny day in April 1933, the "Great McCamey Rattlesnake Derby" was held.

McCamey's Derby may now seem frivolous, but the world was different then. People everywhere were working their way out of global economic disaster. Farmers took bankruptcy. Bankers and brokers jumped from tall buildings. Millions of jobless "rode the rails" in search of work. Bread lines grew longer in the cities.

Next door to Texas, Huey Pierce "The Kingfish" Long urged the nation to "share the wealth — make every man a king." His Populist ideas plus frequent predictions that he would someday be president made the Washington establishment nervous.

Franklin D. Roosevelt was halfway through his "first hundred days" of fundamental change to America's social and financial structure.

Adolf Hitler seized power in Germany. Joseph Stalin liquidated tens of millions of Russians in the name of the "perfect society" to come. Japanese troops marched into a blizzard in China. Franco plotted his way to power in Spain.

Pivotal events of the twentieth century were developing worldwide. People sensed the crumbling of an old order; they sought relaxation from that stress in unconventional ways.

In the Midwest, barnstorming fliers walked the wings of rickety World War I aircraft. Taxi dancing and dance marathons flourished in the cities. Average, law-abiding citizens sought to put spice in their lives by scrounging for bootleg liquor.

Rube Goldberg was alive and well in schemes devised to curb poverty. The intelligentsia endorsed a new idea called technocracy. Technocrats preached that the problem was overproduction. Their solution was to cut the work week to twenty or thirty hours a week, set retirement day at fifty or fifty-five, distribute the same amount of goods to a wider area, and everything would be all right.

The common classes seized on a simpler solution: the chain letter.

Both plans combined the elements of greed and credulity that mark all con games. With an equally firm grasp on unreality, both plans were equally successful.

A Kentucky Derby for rattlesnakes, viewed against the background of its time, seems fairly normal. As Dickens observed about another time of change: "It was the best of times, it was the worst of times."

Talk in coffee shops ran to the spectacular: Clyde Barrow and Bonnie Parker; John Dillinger and Pretty Boy Floyd; ten-cent oil and one-dollar-a-barrel water; the Dean brothers, Paul and Jerome, new pitchers for the St. Louis Cardinals baseball team; Dorothy Lamour, Amelia Earhart, and Snipe Conley's Texon Oilers.

Roustabouts in khakis and women in calico stared bug-eyed at Rattlesnake Brownie's derby setup. "How can he get fifty rattlers off and running at the same time?" they murmured.

Brownie had a way. The collapsible walls of the rattlesnake box, at the appointed time, fulfilled their destiny and collapsed. The simultaneous firing of a Colt .45 revolver signaled to the contestants and their handlers that the race was on.

Without informing the rattlers, Brownie had arranged for a surge of raw electricity to hit the steel box at the same instant. This arrangement provided for an instantaneous elevation of each snake's anti-social quotient by something like 200 points on the hostility scale.

It was sweet pandemonium. To each snake was attached the pole-and-noose harness. To each pole clung a handler. The handler was permitted to prod the creature to change direction; he could not pull or aid the runner.

A mass of muscular, outraged specimens of *crotalus adamanteus* erupted out of the charged box. Handlers dodged snakes while angling their runners into position. Snakes stampeded for any exit available. The crowd yelled for its favorites: "C'mon, Rosie . . . Beat 'em, Esmerelda . . . Run, Drain Pipe . . . Stay in there, V-8. . . ."

The winner was a compact, agile little five-footer who weighed in at four pounds. His name was Slicker; he was a speed demon. Slicker, sponsored by the Owl Drug Store, slipped and slithered his way from the starting box to his designated wicket in four minutes and five seconds. Drain Pipe, entry of Acme Plumbing Company, finished second.

The Great McCamey Rattlesnake Derby was a commercial and artistic success. There was talk of an annual event.

But there has been only one Rattlesnake Derby, the great sporting event of 1933 in the Permian Basin.

Thirty years later, Cuthbert Carll, editor of the *McCamey News* at the time of the derby, spoke fondly of its success.

Asked why, Carll replied: "I told you, there's one guy in every town. Brownie moved to El Paso. It takes a guy like Brownie to pull off a Rattlesnake Derby."

CHAPTER NINE

Oil Man to Trader

The first supply store prospered as Claude Brown found materials in other areas and brought them into McCamey, where they could be sold into the expanding Permian Basin economy. A network of friends and fellow workers fed him leads on equipment available in played-out areas.

Ward County at that time had considerable drilling activity west of McCamey. The tiny town of Grandfalls, twenty miles south of Monahans, became the site of Brown's second supply store. He expanded into New Mexico with a store in Artesia. By 1939 he had six stores, including locations in Crane and Andrews.

The item most in demand, he found, was the working barrel, which is that part of the pump placed in the bottom of the hole. It lifts the oil to the surface.

Most oil wells have three stages in their productive life. First is the "flush" production, which results from natural reservoir pressures without any manmade help. Flush production usually lasts a few weeks. The second, and major, state is that of "settled" production. Properly handled by the operator, settled production can be expected to last a considerable length of time. Production will usually show a long-term, moderately declining output that lasts until the final stage. This stage is called "stripper" production; the well is being "stripped" of its economic value. This phase will last, on a given well, until the amount of oil which can be raised from the ground falls below the cost of production.

Early-day oil fields often experienced wasteful production. A driller would hit a well, produce it wide open as long as it would flow, and when it quit flowing, would go on to the next boom. This philosophy was changing by the mid-thirties.

Brown found a good market for working barrels, balls and seats, sucker rods (which connect the pump at the bottom of the hole to its source of power above ground) and pumping units — all the paraphernalia related to efficient recovery of oil. He built his business on this steady demand.

Brown began buying leases, abandoned wells, working interests, production — anything that could be turned at a profit. His oil field supply business lasted thirty years; it was the nucleus of all his business activities. In May 1966 he sold the business and its stores in McCamey, Crane, and Andrews to Beacon Supply of Pampa. From diversifying into other aspects of the oil industry, Brown moved into a wide range of completely different ventures, from movie making to uranium, from war surplus goods to a used cemetery.

A trader's life is not brimming over with job security. "C. W.,"

First oil field supply store opened in McCamey. Here is Claude Brown, with six-year-old daughter Claudyne, at the store in October 1937.

as he became known in the business world, had his share of "going to the wall" on losing ventures.

There was the gas well in Pecos County, drilled on a contract for U.S. Smelting Company, which blew out and ignited. The fire consumed the rig, the drill pipe, and drill collar. It blew a plume of gas 160 feet into the air.

The call was for Red Adair. "He came out, looked it over and said, 'Get me this, and do that, and I will snub it out,'" Brown recalled. "Then we cried on his shoulder, told him we had to bear the full cost, and he gave us a very large discount. So we have always been big admirers of Red Adair."

Another near-miss involved a boatload of steel pipe, bought in the metal-scarce period after World War II. The pipe was purchased from a dealer in Portland, Oregon, to fill an order from Rodman and Noel in Odessa.

The twelve-inch pipe was used to lay a line carrying casing-head gas (the gas produced from an oil well, not the gas that flows out of a gas well). The line ran from northwest of Odessa to a point south of Odessa, both points in Ector County.

"This was after the war. Pipe was scarce, and if they could have bought new pipe they would have gotten it in the first place. When the pipe got to Odessa and they laid the line . . ." Brown shuddered at the memory, "there were so many pin holes in it that they actually used wooden pegs to plug the line."

If the buyer had turned down the pipe, Brown said, "It would probably have been the end of C. W. Brown Pipe and Supply Company, for I was dealing in anything and everything, and my finances were very weak at the time."

Another deal that almost took Brown under involved a boatload of steel tanks, bound for the Philippine Islands but never used due to the end of World War II. Brown put down $50,000 as deposit against a purchase price of $750,000. He figured to make a profit of perhaps $250,000.

The boatload of surplus 100-barrel and 250–barrel tanks was shipped to Houston for inspection and delivery. Financing had been arranged; taking delivery involved only inspection and writing a check.

"As good as new" had been the sales pitch. Unfortunately, the tanks had been offloaded in the Philippines too close to the ocean. Salt water had corroded the bottom seals.

Brown had brought along his attorney, Jim Langdon, "just in case."

"I had a fight on my hands over that boatload of tanks," Brown said. "We spent one week in the Rice Hotel. I will never forget it; we spent all one night putting quarters in a pay radio in our room, listening to the election, when Harry Truman was elected president. Papers were on the streets announcing Dewey's election. That news changed during the night.

"We had to whip them down and get back my deposit of $50,000. If I had been compelled to pay up on my contract, it would surely have been the last of my business."

Brown bought 450 searchlights from the U.S. Army. Each light came with a GE portable electric generator. Most of them went to the Sprayberry field, where they were popular items with drilling contractors. He sold a dozen lights to a Texas merchant who used them to advertise store openings in Dallas, Fort Worth, Houston, and San Antonio.

Trader Brown supplied a portion of Lubbock County's irrigation equipment. He bought and sold four million feet of "invasion pipe." The Lone Star Gas line from Eden to Miles came from the Brown stockpile.

One of his best deals arose from the wartime shortage of transportation. Brown was running six cable-tool rigs in Crockett County. Transportation became so scarce that he was forced to build a camp on the drilling lease. His drilling crews and tool dressers stayed at the camp. Hauling them to the job site was part of the hiring process.

"I had hounded my friend Bill Edwards about getting a new car, a truck, a pickup or any kind of vehicle. So much, in fact, that we had almost become enemies.

"Finally, one day Edwards said, 'When the government lets the motor companies start back to producing cars and trucks, I will make everyone so mad over who to serve first, that I am just about ready to quit the car business. For just a little bit, I'd sell out.'"

Brown joked in return, "For just a little bit, I'd buy you out."

When Brown arrived at his office next morning Bill Edwards, the General Motors dealer, sat there waiting for him. The two men made a handshake deal that put C. W. Brown into the car dealership business for the next thirty-five years.

"I agreed on a price, not knowing that you had to go through a lot of red tape with GM before they would approve you as a dealer. With the help of my good friend Mr. Ulmer and the First National Bank of Midland, I became a car dealer."

Brown kept trading, playing the cards he was dealt, making the most of every situation.

CHAPTER TEN

Claudyne

Claudyne Brown enrolled as a freshman at Southern Methodist University in 1948. En route to Austin one summer day, she stopped at her father's office to say goodbye.

Claude Brown had a visitor, a young geologist from Louisiana State University who was "sitting on a well" near McCamey for his employer, Union Sulphur & Oil Company. He introduced Ed Thorp to his daughter. Claudyne drove on to Austin.

Thorp returned to his home in Lake Charles; Claudyne went to school in Dallas. The two began a long-range courtship. They married in the First Methodist Church of McCamey December 15, 1950.

"It is hard for partners to get along, but when a partnership succeeds with the partners being father-in-law and son-in-law, it is one for the books," Brown declared.

Brown, the resourceful veteran, and Thorp, a geology graduate of LSU, represented two distinct types in the oil business. Entirely a self-made man, Brown had worked his way to the top by ingenuity, some daring, an instinct for timing, and sheer hard work.

Thorp represented the wave of the future in what had become, during the twentieth century, the world's biggest business.

Six months later Thorp left Union Sulphur & Oil. He and Claude Brown formed the Brown & Thorp Oil and Drilling Company.

Brown & Thorp brought in the Girvin Field, the Owega Field

in Pecos County, and the Brown and Thorp Field. At the same time, C. W. pursued his own non-oil ventures.

Ed Thorp persuaded his friend Keith Somerville, geologist from West Virginia, to join the firm in McCamey. Somerville married Hazel Babb in McCamey and later became a very successful independent geologist in Midland.

Brown & Thorp operated a drilling firm that grew to eleven cable-tool rigs and five rotary rigs. At its peak it employed 115 workers.

The oil company deals grew larger. In 1954 Brown & Thorp sold a group of fifty-four wells in Pecos County to McAlester Fuel for $2.7 million.

In the oil business, one thing leads to another. The Brown & Thorp Girvin Field had been discovered, but Brown & Thorp had no market. A deal was made with Crown Central Petroleum Company, of Houston, to lay a sixty-five-mile gathering system. The system was later expanded to 125 miles, the Girvin Field oil thus winding up in steel tanks in Houston.

The company was briefly in and out of the uranium business. Beginning in the 1950s, worldwide demand grew for uranium. Brown & Thorp acquired a lease on 450,000 acres in New Mexico, which they sold in a cash-and-stock deal during a period of trading oil properties.

A chance encounter in an elevator in Dallas led to a revival of Brown's thirty-year-old friendship with John Turner — and a multi-million-dollar deal. Ed and Claudyne Thorp were attending a meeting of the Mid-Continent Oil & Gas Association in Dallas. Turner, on the elevator with the couple, saw Claudyne's name tag.

"I have a friend of thirty years ago in McCamey, name of C. W. Brown," Turner said by way of introduction.

"He is my father," Claudyne replied. The result of that meeting was related in May 1972 in Brown's speech to the Permian Basin Pioneers Association in Midland:

> Ed and Claudyne and Turner visited in the hotel lobby. Turner told them he was trying to sell 125 wells in the Panhandle for five and one-half million dollars. Ed Thorp went to Borger from Dallas. Brown & Thorp began negotiating; we bought the 125 wells for four and one-half million cash. We drilled five more wells. A year later we sold the field for five and one-half million.

We financed all of our four and one-half million; did not put a nickel of our own money in the deal, even the down payment.

I ran into John Turner last week in Dallas. He tells me that since I bought him out he has taken one and one-half million profit in Pacific Petroleum Company stock and has a million profit in American Petrofina stock, if he wanted to sell.

The moral is, it just shows what can be done under the free enterprise system, when two roustabouts can do this. One finished the eighth grade and the other one finished high school.

In real estate, as in oil, Claude Brown was an innovator. "I have always been able to sell almost anything over the past fifty years, but I have two used churches in McCamey, one used bank in Fort Stockton, and one abandoned cemetery that I have found no takers on."

Unusual trades were his trademark. Brown figured that he had helped on the construction of every church building in McCamey, either through cash donation, gift of land, or providing material.

First Christian and Presbyterian churches in McCamey look alike for a reason. Brown bought a truckload of brick for the First Christian Church; he gave the leftover brick to the Presbyterians for their building program.

Brown bought the old Methodist Church in McCamey and gave the church a lot for a new building. Brown & Thorp also donated $40,000. When Jim Langdon was appointed to the Texas Railroad Commission and moved to Austin, he put a bank building in Fort Stockton on the market. Brown bought the bank building and sold it to a furniture company.

"We bought 230 acres on Loop 820 on the east side of Fort Worth," he said. "The land had an old family cemetery on it with about twenty-five graves in it. We sold this to Mike Myers of Dallas and he has filled the land with apartment buildings. He just built a wall around the cemetery. There was no ingress or regress to the property; my lawyer says it was impossible to move the bodies, so we just threw the cemetery in."

Brown & Thorp constructed 352 apartments in Fort Worth and Beaumont. Brown said in 1972 he considered the investment "just as good as an offset to a prolific Gomez gas well." Brown & Thorp bought twenty sections of ranch land in Pecos County;

their sheep and goat operation there showed more losses than gains. Through the years Brown acquired 1,300 acres of land bordering McCamey.

Eyesores left from previous booms are a common sight in many Texas oil towns. There are a few in McCamey, but far fewer than there would have been had Brown not practiced his own version of urban renewal. During his lifetime, he bought and razed more than fifteen old hotels and other two-story buildings that had been thrown up during boom times.

During Brown's tenure as mayor of McCamey (1949–1954), 100 blocks of paved streets were added. The city built a new city hall, fire station, and jail. The water and sewer systems were improved, and the main highway through McCamey was widened. These improvements were made at the same time the city's debt was gradually reduced.

In 1957 Claude Brown received the first "Mr. McCamey" award. He placed the bronze plaque in his office beside the picture of his first grandson, Claude Wilson Thorp.

In December 1968 Claude and Christine Brown's world turned upside down. Claudyne Thorp, in her Beaumont home, complained of a headache. Her children came home from school to find their mother collapsed in the hall. The next day Claudyne was dead, victim of a vicious brain tumor. She was thirty-seven years old, mother of two boys and two girls: Claude Wilson, Terry, Christy, and Jim.

"Claudyne was our inspiration," Claude said quietly. "She kept this family venture on the go. All we can do now is try to help the grandchildren, doing what we think she would want."

Elected president of the West Texas Chamber of Commerce in 1972, Brown paid tribute to his daughter: "I dedicate this year of my service to her memory."

CHAPTER ELEVEN

The Methodist Church

Texas is a great, beautiful, dry, windy,
Methodist, live-oak State.
                    —Josiah W. Whipple, 1843

What about God?

This question hung in the balance through the nineteenth century, as America defined itself and its destiny.

By 1800 America was spilling through the Cumberland Gap into Kentucky, Tennessee, Ohio, Indiana, Michigan, and Wisconsin. J. Hector St. John Crevecoeur, in 1781, had already perceived the American as a chronic "mover."[1]

Which way would the West go? Would its representatives crush old institutions in the East? Would it become a shaggy, unchurched world of loose morals and corn liquor, where marriages were celebrated long after children had arrived? Would the West worship God?

Even in 1800 the young nation seemed to sense that the West held the key to America's future.

The East, however, was borrowing trouble. Westerners, with three centuries of stern Protestantism behind them, knew they needed God. Religion offered what the pioneer was staking his life on: a bright shining future beyond the perilous present, a present in which the fatal germ, the unexpected arrow, was always just around the corner. The catch was that the West intended to be saved the way it did everything else: on its own individualistic, democratic terms.

Confusion was a luxury the frontier could not afford. Westerners rebelled against complex theological rules. They trusted aristocracy in the church leadership about as much as they trusted the Indian. They wanted cheap land, the vote, and a simple form of salvation.

In the world of 1800 the individual, not society, had become the bottom line. Westerners demanded, and got, a religion that was simple, practical, and relevant to the fundamental context of each man's life.

Fundamentalism thus became the religion of the West. The dramatic, exuberant camp meeting became its stage.

The essence of fundamentalism is simplicity of form and confidence of spirit. The bedrock of its faith is the belief that virtue will be rewarded and vice will be punished. Righteousness is a shield against the enemy—but each man should keep his powder dry.

Conservative Presbyterians, Episcopalians, and Congregationalists on the East Coast frowned on the emotional preaching of revivals. How could enthusiasm replace an educated clergy for discerning how God winnows his flock? Fundamentalism threatened the status quo. The whole orderly scheme of life on earth, the straight and narrow gate of salvation, stood in peril.

At this time the Methodist Church stepped forward.

The Wesleyans, a religious society within the Church of England, had lacked both members and money in the colonies during the American Revolution, when "the minds of men were full of sin and politics."[2] Francis Asbury, John Wesley's superintendent, organized the Methodist Episcopal Church of America at the Baltimore Conference in 1784. He appointed himself its first bishop and circuit rider. For the next five years he rode horseback 5,000 miles a year in ministering to Methodists in lonely settlements.

Methodists took the lead in evangelizing the frontier. Not all worshipers favored its enthusiastic style. In Texas, Stephen F. Austin eschewed "the Methodist excitement," but the Methodist Church early established itself as the Protestant leader across the Appalachians. By 1820, Methodists had held 1,000 camp meetings in the West.

With a plain-spoken ministry and no claims of limited election to salvation, the Methodist Church was in the right place at the right time, teaching what frontier people needed to hear, justifying the harsh things men had to do in order to survive.

Mexico required that immigrants moving into colonial Texas must affirm loyalty to the Roman Catholic Church. Once the colonist had sworn allegiance to the church, however, he was free to follow his own religious inclinations.

Stephen F. Austin respected the Roman Catholic Church and expected members of the Austin Colony to do the same. Austin appealed several times to the Mexican government for a priest to perform weddings and baptisms in the colony, but Mexican clergymen made infrequent visits north of the Rio Grande. In 1841 a young preacher in Illinois was appointed "foreign missionary" to the Republic of Texas. Josiah W. Whipple kissed his mother, mounted his horse, and set out to spread the gospel.

Riding his circuit in the Republic of Texas, Whipple knew he had done well to obey the bishop's call; Texas obviously needed his ministry. His journal entry in Austin on February 13, 1842, is fervent: "May God in mercy send by whom he will, but send salvation to this wicked town."[3]

Methodist circuit riders continued to trickle across the Red and the Sabine rivers. They preached the gospel; they also honed their skills in the expedients of frontier life. They learned to sleep on the ground, to build rafts and cross swollen streams, and to bury men they stumbled across who had frozen to death in the latest norther.

The best-known circuit rider in Texas was Andrew Jackson Potter, "fighting parson."[4] Potter, born in Missouri in 1830, was a hard-drinking Indian fighter known on the frontier for his courage and marksmanship. In 1856 he wandered into a camp meeting near San Antonio. He experienced a conversion and thence went forth to fight God's battles, his pugnacious nature harmonizing nicely with the militant measures of Christianity. Potter was a natural leader of men. With a Bible in his left hand and a six-shooter in his right, he went about doing the Lord's work in the devil's backyard of Texas saloons, poker games, and horse races.

If wildcatters and roustabouts moved west, could women and children be far behind? Despite the universal agreement that "Texas was hell on women and horses," women and children soon appeared in every boomtown in Texas. Churches and schools followed.

On the second Sunday in June of 1927, thirteen McCamey men and women met in the old Queen Theater on Fifth Street. They organized the First Methodist Church.

McCamey in 1927 had dirt streets and plank sidewalks. Many people lived in tents. But enthusiasm dies hard on the frontier. Sunday school teachers assembled the town's children every Sunday morning and marched them down Main Street singing hymns. Roughnecks removed their hats as the children passed by.

The year 1945 was a watershed year for the twentieth century. World War II veterans observed that when they entered the service in 1941, it was a much different world from the one they would find when they returned in 1945.

The year was a turning point as well for Claude Brown. Dr. C. Jordan Mann, pastor of the First Methodist Church of McCamey, remembers: "Claude joined the church in 1945. We moved to McCamey in 1947. What amazed me was his faithful relationship to the church, his constant and steady attendance and concern for her welfare—locally and in the total church—and to discover that he had joined only two years before. He finally had both the time and the means to enter into full service in the church."

"Things started breaking right for me," Brown told Pastor Mann. "The Lord has blessed me. I decided I ought to do the right thing with my money."

It was the beginning of a more abundant life.

World War II years had brought a season of profit to the Permian Basin. The Texas Railroad Commission, which had earlier curtailed production in order to maintain a supply/demand balance, changed its policy to all-out production.

When World War II ended, Claude Brown, a man of modest tastes, found himself headed for rich-oil-man stature.

In one of the moves that defined his life, Brown began looking for ways to bestow some blessings. "I don't have any money," he would say to petitioners in later years. "I gave it all away."

The first object of his humanitarian instincts was the Methodist Church. When Brown entered the church he began to study, to pray, and to try to live by the teachings of the church.

Marion Brown, younger brother of Claude, in England in 1944, six weeks before D-Day.

C. W. Brown and brother Marion (left) at Marion's home in Albuquerque, New Mexico.

"Life has simple rules," he said years later. "All the rules are there in the Bible, if a person will just read them."

Brown offered his talents to the church. He served as a director of the Methodist Foundation in Austin and as a trustee of the Methodist Mission Home in San Antonio. He acted as Southwest Conference delegate to General Conferences of the United Methodist Church in Pittsburgh, Chicago, Dallas, and Oklahoma City. At the U.S. General Conventions he met Methodists from all over the world.

When McCamey Methodists voted to build a new church, Brown, then chairman of the official board, donated two acres east of the Iraan highway for the building site. In a board meeting of August 22, 1957, Brown offered to buy the old church property and to assume the $8,500 debt on the parsonage. The board voted to accept his offer.

Methodists saw education of the clergy as crucial to the church's mission. In 1966 Brown excused himself from Christmas dinner to write a check for $12,500. The gift would fund the Ed Robb Evangelical Foundation and create fellowship grants for seminary students.

Brown discerned a similarity in the objectives of religion and politics: the general improvement of the human condition. Prosperity in business financed his convictions. In 1966, after serving on McMurry College Board of Regents, Brown donated $100,000 to the college's endowment program. His gift would underwrite the Claude Brown Symposium on Texas Politics, an annual gathering "to inform and educate the people of Texas on the practical aspects of politics." Attorney General John Ben Shepperd was keynote speaker for the first symposium at McMurry College December 7, 1967.

"Had a good year," Brown said, his eyes twinkling.

McMurry College awarded Brown an honorary doctor of humane letters degree in 1968.

"A man with Claude's spirit, his attitude, and his activity must require faith . . . in men and faith in the eternal order of things," mused Judge Tom Reavely, 167th District Court.

"Claude took genuine pleasure in using his money for his friends," Jordan Mann recalled. "We never articulated this, but his thinking about his money, I would say, was like this: 'I have the money. We are not equal in this; I have more. So I shall use it for both of us. Remember that a joy that's shared is a joy made double.' "

There were more good years to come.

Descent into the airport did not last long. Jagged, purple peaks of the Andes soon rose up to meet them. Below, spread over the slopes and valley at 12,000 feet, La Paz slumbered in its afternoon siesta.

Claude Brown and his six Methodist companions – Dr. Ted Richardson; Dr. John T. King, president of Huston-Tillotson College; James Walker; James Morris; Jack McQueen; and Judge Tom Reavely – stepped out of the Braniff plane into another world: Bolivia. It was 1967.

John Wesley himself had pointed the way: "My parish is the world."

Brown first heard about the church's work in Bolivia at the Methodist General Conference in Pittsburgh in 1964. Reavely and Walker had visited the Bolivian mission in 1962. Their discussions about it had whetted Brown's interest.

"So in 1967 they rounded up seven of us laymen for a ten-day trip to see the work of the Methodist Church and its missionaries," Brown explained. In addition to personal luggage, the travelers took items their missionaries had requested: calculator, adding machine, amplifier for ham radio station, and two suitcases of children's clothing.

In Lima, Peru, the men missed their plane connection to La Paz by thirty minutes. They cleared customs with their luggage and went into Lima's Hotel Bolivia to wait for the next flight twenty-four hours later.

"Everyone in Peru and Bolivia assured us that this was the first time in history a Braniff flight had been on time, and it had to be the time we needed it to be late!" Brown recalled. "Paul McCleary and his people were to meet us at the airport in La Paz, but there was no way to call and let them know we would be a day late." Welcome to Latin America in the sixties.

The Texans chartered a limousine and spent the day sightseeing. They learned that Peru has a largely agrarian economy, untapped natural resources, and a vast gap between rich and poor.

"One fact we learned about Peru was that its government

spent twice what it took in last year in taxes," Brown said. "This made an American feel at home right away."

In La Paz the laymen were met by their missionaries: Paul McCleary, executive secretary of the Methodist Church in Bolivia, and his four children; Nova Dickson, counselor of the American Institute, Cochabamba, and her son George; and Lucho Zalles, U.S.-educated Bolivian who represented Gulf Oil in Bolivia.

The visitors suggested lunch for the group. In the dining room, a frosty maitre d' complained to Mrs. Dickson that one of the American gentlemen was not wearing a tie. The object of his complaint was Claude Brown.

"Don't mind him." Nova Dickson waved her hand in a dismissive gesture. "He's just an oil man. He doesn't mean anything by it." Brown picked up the check for lunch for fourteen people. It came to $14.25.

For the next ten days the Texans looked and listened in Cochabamba, Santa Cruz, and La Paz, at 12,000 feet the world's highest city. They found in Bolivia a tense, brooding land rich in resources of tin, gold and silver, debilitated by 400 years of feudalism. Women in bowler hats and great colorful skirts, babies strapped to their backs, appeared to form the backbone of the economy. They streamed into the *mercado* before dawn, marketing their papayas and mangoes with the feverish intensity of commodity brokers on the floor of the Chicago Board of Trade.

The Texan visitors saw a country with modern buildings, poor transportation, and a per capita average income of less than $100. They visited American Methodists teaching in schools, working in clinics, and preaching in churches. In Clinica Americana they met Juanita Ortiz, a seventeen-year-old Indian girl who had been in bed two years and passed the hours knitting for other people. Juanita had had two operations; she needed another one that would cost $450 (including hospital stay). The Texans quickly made up the amount and left it with Paul McCleary, telling him to see her through and to keep them informed on her progress.

Dr. T. F. Thompson, a young Canadian missionary, managed the hospital.

In Santa Cruz, the ancient capital in eastern Bolivia, they found tropical jungle landscape with blowing sand. "Looks like Monahans before pavement," Brown remarked. "They use jeeps for taxis on account of sand and no pavement." Here the group met Sandy White, a graduate of Texas A&M from Stephenville who headed the U.S. and British aid to Bolivia.

"The day we were there everybody was excited about a load of twenty heifers due to arrive from Indiana," Brown remembered. "This project puts the cow into the hands of a committee. The committee decides who gets the cow and keeps an eye out to see that the cow is cared for. The first calf is given back, then doled out by the committee to yet another farmer. The process goes on, not only with cows but with other livestock as well."

They saw undernourished children receiving vitamins; teenaged boys planting beets; men learning to lead and tame heifers rather than beat the cows into submission every night before milking.

The laymen found, on every hand, evidence of the "church in the world," so identified with humanity's struggle that it could hardly be measured or placed in a particular location. They found that the Southwest Texas Conference, having adopted Bolivia as its protégé, had made its mark in the austere country. Methodist money and manpower abetted the climate of incipient freedom.

Lucho Zalles wanted to go into the chicken business. He explained to the Texans how much profit he figured he could make. The only hitch in his plan was capital for seed money; it would cost $10,000 to get the business started.

Claude Brown and Judge Reavely considered Lucho's plan, looked at each other, nodded. They financed Lucho with a no-interest loan of $10,000.

Lucho repaid the loan in small amounts as he was able, but the chicken business ultimately lost more money than it made. Years later, after Lucho's death, Brown and Reavely instructed Lucho's estate to forget the balance of the note.

"Some of my schemes were a mistake from the word go," Brown laughed. "Such as the movie industry, the sheep business, and raising chickens."

Bolivia continued slowly to strengthen its infrastructure. Claude Brown was pleased to play a part in the country's progress.

Brown would be glad in years to come that he met attractive widow Nova Dickson. The next time they saw each other was in 1990 at Methodist Conference in San Antonio. They married March 30, 1991, in Kerrville.

CHAPTER TWELVE

Democratic Party

Four compass points defined Claude Brown's life: home, the Methodist Church, the oil business, and the Democratic Party.

The man called Mr. McCamey was an unreconstructed "Sam Rayburn Democrat." He maintained that he was "a conservative Democrat, a lot more conservative than some of my Republican friends."

Brown relished the nuts-and-bolts machinery of politics, from precinct to national levels. Throughout his six decades of political involvement, from the turbulent thirties to the uneasy eighties, he participated fully in the democratic process. He witnessed epochal changes in Texas politics.

The state of Texas went from an agrarian to an industrial economy, from a rural to an urban society, from limited to full enfranchisement at the polls. Texas also moved from a brass-collar de facto one-party state to a two-party system.

Brown's credentials as a political observer included four trips to the Democratic National Convention as a delegate from Upton County, his presence constituting fifty percent of Upton County's total representation. He held state and county party offices and followed politics assiduously at all levels.

He also enjoyed a personal friendship with eight governors of Texas, from 1950 to 1992. His memories and opinions weave a tapestry of the Lone Star State in the last half of the twentieth century.

Allan Shivers, then lieutenant governor, became governor by

Claude Brown in Washington, D.C., in 1960.

succession in July 1949, on the death of Governor Beauford Jester. Shivers sought and won three full two-year terms, from 1950 to 1956. The state was firmly controlled by conservative Democrats.

The "tidelands issue" divided Texas Democrats from the national party in 1952. Texas tidelands, the offshore lands bordering on the 380 miles of Texas coastline, were considered to contain valuable reserves of petroleum.

Shivers led the Eisenhower revolt, which helped put the World War II hero-general in the White House. Eisenhower permitted Texas to keep its oil-rich tidelands, the first twelve miles offshore in the Gulf of Mexico.

Brown learned in 1952 how ferocious the political trenches can become. His friend Shivers had won his first term as governor in 1950. The overheated election year of 1952 was dominated by the issue of the Texas tidelands. Federal officials had staked their verbal claims to these lands three years earlier.

Candidates for president in 1952 were Gen. Dwight D. Eisenhower, Republican, and Democrat Adlai E. Stevenson. Governor Shivers contacted candidate Stevenson to sound out his position on the tidelands question: "Who owns the tidelands? The state of Texas or the federal government?"

Shivers was not satisfied with Stevenson's response. The governor returned to Texas and helped to form a "Democrats for Eisenhower" drive to campaign for Ike in the fall. Overwhelmingly Democratic in national and local politics, Texas voters were largely conservative in their views — which meant that they preferred Ike to Adlai.

To some members of the Democratic Party, however, Governor Shivers had gone too far. He and his followers were labeled "Shivercrats." Sell-out charges surfaced, and rhetoric escalated to shrill new levels.

Brown backed Shivers in the controversy, as did most oil men in Texas. "I put out his posters all over McCamey," he recalled, "and the next day they were all torn down. The old-line Democrats thought he was trying to turn Republican." He thought for a moment. "My experience has been that the North and the East Coast are not a bit concerned about the welfare of Texas.

"All in all, I think Allan Shivers made a very fine, dignified, conservative governor of Texas. I had him as a friend the balance of his career, a fact of which I am proud. Governor Shivers had a charming first lady, from a prominent early-day South Texas family."

The fifties and sixties were good to Texas economically, a period of rapid industrial growth. Petroleum, Texas' basic industry, moved over to make room for defense-related manufacturing plants, aluminum and high-tech start-up companies.

Jack Kilby, an engineer at Texas Instruments in Dallas, developed the transistor micro-chip. This device became the "brain" of the computer that has revolutionized many dimensions of life: manufacturing, communications, politics, education, and finance. TI is an offshoot of the oil business; it started as a seismograph-based operation aimed at mapping the earth's underground in the search for oil.

Price Daniel was governor of Texas from 1956 to 1962. Governor Daniel's Baylor University law school classmate, Jim Langdon, later moved to McCamey and became Claude Brown's attorney.

"Price Daniel was a very successful governor," Brown recalled, "and had a charming wife who was a descendant of Sam Houston. She was probably the most dignified first lady Texas has had."

As mayor of McCamey, Claude Brown promoted an airport for the city. In 1947 McCamey became a stop on the Trans-Texas Airline route from Fort Worth to Brownwood, San Angelo, Fort Stockton, Marfa, and later, during the heyday of Billie Sol Estes,

Claude and Christine Brown at Democratic National Convention in Atlantic City in 1964.

Pecos. Brown's daughter Claudyne and her SMU roommate, Dorothy Ann (Dot) Borders, came out on the first TTA flight. After the dedication Dot and Claudyne flew on to Marfa and Pecos. At Pecos, Brown's brother Marion and their mother, Hattie Lee, boarded the plane and returned to McCamey for a visit.

Betty Ewan of Midland recalls the spring afternoon Claudyne's mother called her at SMU. "Meet the Trans-Texas plane that gets to Love Field at four. Leola cooked something special today and we're sending you some." Betty, Claudyne, and Dot met the plane and soon feasted on Leola Curry's fried chicken and coleslaw. Leola worked as the Browns' housekeeper forty-two years.

Trans-Texas sent its Washington lawyer on the first flight to McCamey. Claude Brown was favorably impressed by the young man named John Connally.

"He was an unknown then," Brown recalled years later. "After the dedication of the McCamey Airport, he went on to be a part of Lyndon B. Johnson's team. And then LBJ, Sam Rayburn, and Sid Richardson decided Connally had a political future. Sid Richardson brought him into Fort Worth with the Richardson and Bass enterprises, and the rest is well known."

Connally governed Texas from 1962 to 1968, through years of national and international tension.

"He was a governor with the drive to get things accomplished for the state and the U.S.," was Brown's evaluation. "He was among the tops in Texas government. John always had the future of Texas on his mind. There were others with much ability, but Big John had that extra push to get things accomplished for the state and for the U.S."

Brown was among a small group of Connally's friends who talked him into running for governor of Texas. Others who gathered at the Texas Hotel in Fort Worth to encourage Connally included Perry Bass, Tom Sealy, Bob Strauss, Jake Pickle, Frank Irwin, and Sid Richardson.

Connally became even more famous during his term as a wounded survivor of the John F. Kennedy assassination in Dallas on November 22, 1963. When the shots were fired, Brown was in the Baker Hotel with other Democratic chieftains, preparing to welcome President Kennedy to Texas.

Governor Connally appointed Brown to the Texas State Industrial Commission, a post Brown held six years. Brown pointed out that Governor Connally, having witnessed the effects of industry at Massachusetts Institute of Technology and in California's Silicon Valley, worked to bring industry into agrarian Texas. And he did so, Brown added, "on a very small budget of less than five hundred thousand dollars a year. Now the budget is in the billions."

Permian Basin oil men decided to create a Petroleum Museum during Connally's term as governor. Republican George Abell and his attorney, Maurice Bullock, did the groundwork. When the time came to request a charter for the museum, they turned to their good friend, Democrat Claude Brown.

"The museum's charter was granted right away," Bullock recalls. "In the office of John Hill, Texas secretary of state. It was October 2, 1967."[1]

Brown demonstrated his affection for the younger man in 1993, only months before his own death. Against his physician's advice, Brown had his secretary, Brenda Mitchell, drive him over 300 miles from McCamey to Austin for John Connally's funeral.

One truism in life is that a man often admires most in others the traits he himself possesses. Preston Smith, governor of Texas from 1968 to 1972, was a favorite political figure for Claude Brown.

Smith grew up in West Texas, as did Brown. He worked his way up through the ranks of the Democratic Party, as did Brown. His leadership style was down-to-earth, a bit homey, and he cultivated friends at all levels of society.

"I wish we had more like him today," Brown said in 1993.

For the state of Texas, Smith's two terms of two years each were years of rapid urbanization. Texas was rocked politically by scandals, the worst in Texas since the days of Ma and Pa Ferguson in the 1930s. A bribery charge involving Houston banker Frank Sharp brought down Speaker of the Texas House of Representatives Gus Mutscher. Population figures of the 1970 census revealed the shift from a sparsely settled state to an urban state: the population exceeded eleven million, placing Texas in sixth place nationally. Houston, Dallas, and San Antonio were among the ten largest cities in the United States.

More significant for Brown's world was the fact that in 1970 the amount of oil and gas produced annually in the U.S. peaked. (Since then it has steadily declined.)

The international oil industry would create the economic and political focus for the mid-1970s. The Organization of Petro-

Texas Secretary of State John Hill issues charter for the Permian Basin Petroleum Museum, October 2, 1966. From left: George Abell, Hill, Maurice R. Bullock, and Claude Brown.

C. J. Kelly, left, president of Midland National Bank, confers with Brown on West Texas Chamber of Commerce business.

Conventioneers Claude and Christine Brown in El Paso. Brown was president of the West Texas Chamber of Commerce.

leum Exporting Countries rattled its armor and shook founda-
tions all the way to McCamey when, in 1973, it boycotted the
American market. Energy prices shot skyward. The immediate
effect was inflationary; the lasting effect has been uncertainty.

Now that the U.S. could not count on the availability of cheap
foreign oil, the independent producer assumed a new importance.
In the Permian Basin, wildcatting rose 21.6 percent in 1974, 12
percent in 1975, and 6.3 percent in 1976.

Claude Brown was one of thirty-six individuals who met in
the board room of the Uvalde State Bank to select a gubernato-
rial candidate for the 1972-1974 term. The hometown product
they selected, Dolph Briscoe, would have a turbulent tour of duty
in Austin.

In the summer of 1972 Claude Brown served as delegate to
the Democratic National Convention in Miami Beach, Florida.
Senator George McGovern came from a five percent chance six
months earlier to be elected Democratic nominee on the first
ballot. Brown's comment on McGovern's candidacy reveals something of the Texan's own habits.

"Someone asked me how Senator George McGovern accomplished all this in so short a time. My answer was 'How do you
think I have been a delegate to four national conventions from
Upton County, which has only two votes out of the thirty-seven
counties in the twenty-fifth senatorial district? We compete with
Midland, San Angelo, Fort Stockton, Monahans, Uvalde, and New
Braunfels. You just work behind the scene while the other fellow
is asleep.'"

The OPEC-created energy crisis brought inflation and
triggered economic problems in other industries. Drilling costs
increased. Interest rates rose with inflation from 10.8 percent in
1974 to 18.8 percent in 1981.

Dolph Briscoe had to deal not only with inflation but with
the virulent reformist syndrome abroad in the land following the
Sharpstown and Watergate scandals. Governor Briscoe had his
plate full, according to Claude Brown:

"Dolph Briscoe was much like Governor Preston Smith in
being a down-to-earth man. He knew family values and lived by
them. He improved our educational system, our rural roads, and
made progress on screwworm eradication. He was also a big
worker in Boy Scouts."

When William P. (Bill) Clements came out of Southern Methodist University and went to the oil fields, his first drilling job was on the Tippett ranch, seven miles outside of McCamey. "The best time I have ever had in my life was living in a trailer by that drilling rig on the Tippett ranch and hunting quail," Clements said.

Clements and Brown had quail hunting and the oil business as common interests. They were, however, on opposite sides politically. Clements narrowly defeated John Hill, the Democratic candidate, in a close race in the 1978 election. He became the first Republican governor of Texas since post-Civil War Reconstruction days — more than a century.

"Bill Clements and I belong to different political parties, but I admire him and consider him a friend," Brown said. "He had some good programs in his term, was a little harsh on U.S. Democrats, but I still call him my friend."

Clements made Texas political history in 1978 when he became the first Republican governor since Reconstruction. After losing in 1982, he made a comeback and won again in 1986.

The eighties evoked extreme commercial and economic volatility. Texas became less reliant on its energy industry and began moving into high-tech areas.

Radical sociological changes in Texas in the second half of the twentieth century shaped the outcome of the 1986 campaign between Clements and Mark White. Election returns informed voters that Texas was no longer a one-party state.

Victory for Republican Clements was in itself significant. But even more telling was the voter breakdown. Republican Party candidates historically ran strongest in large cities and lost elections in small towns and rural areas. In 1986 Clements beat White in rural and small towns, and carried only two of the state's major urban areas.

Brown regarded Mark White as a good governor, mainly interested in education.

Ann Richards defeated oil man Clayton Williams after her opponent, an unlikely politician, made some costly gaffes trying to ad-lib in the Texas governor's race. Governor Richards knows the political game, but she may have not fully utilized one of her potential assets in her 1990 campaign.

Elder statesman Brown, whose Democratic Party credentials were somewhat longer than the average Russian novel, had hoped to receive a statewide assignment in Richards' campaign against

Politickin' with John and Nellie Connally.

Politickin' with Ann Richards.

Williams. After her election, Richards informed Brown that she wanted him to be "my man in Upton County" (population 5,600; registered voters, 1,400).

"I guess I overestimated my worth to Ann," Brown observed wistfully. "Anyway, my friend Clayton would not keep quiet, so Ann was elected and she is my governor now (1993)."

Brown's interest in the political process stemmed from his concern for individual hardship. "I always said, even as a young man, that if and when I had the ability, I would try to do something for the other fellow. I wanted to help the Masonic Lodge and the Methodist Church in particular."

One catalyst for his political activities was his association with Jim Langdon. One of McCamey's first lawyers, Langdon, later to become chairman of the Texas Railroad Commission, moved to McCamey in January 1946 with a bride, a four-month-old son, and little else. C. W. Brown became Langdon's first client; the two followed the world of politics together.

Three governors considered Brown for nomination to the Texas Railroad Commission, which regulates the production of oil and gas for the state. As the nation's largest producer of hydrocarbons, Texas has long been acutely aware of the problems inherent in the extreme volatility of production and prices. The discovery well in October 1926 of the famous Yates Field in Pecos County was the turning point for unlimited production. Transcontinental Oil Company, owned by Mike Benedum and Joe Trees, opened up an enormous field with the Yates discovery twenty-five miles south of the McCamey Field. They drilled wells with a potential of almost 170,000 barrels a day.

Production of this scale — coupled with inadequate storage and pipeline facilities — could mean depressed prices, and depressed prices meant disaster to the small, independent producer. Economic disaster was averted when producers agreed on voluntary proration, a program that had limited success. After Dad Joiner's discovery of the giant East Texas Field in 1930, oil flooded the market and prices fell. Violence in the oil patch led first to martial law, then to state regulation of the oil industry. The Texas Railroad Commission has become a model for other states and several nations.

Claude Brown's desire to serve as chairman of the Railroad Commission was never realized. He was three times a bridesmaid but never a bride: in the 1960s, when Governor Connally appointed Jim Langdon; again, a few years later, when Governor Briscoe appointed Mac Wallace; and most recently when Governor Richards named Mary Scott Nabors to the post.

Believing as he did that each individual should become active in his community, Claude Brown was deeply involved in politics by 1950. The personal, ground-level theater of politics found a willing recruit and a lifelong aficionado in the "roustabout from McCamey."

Politics is a home for the gregarious, which was C. W. Brown from hat to socks. He did not delve into the intellectual or philosophical side of either politics or business. ("The Texan mentality is intelligent, but utterly unintellectual," according to historian T. R. Fehrenbach.) Politics to Claude Brown meant people. When he was asked which of his own abilities he valued most, he replied, "I pride myself that I know people."

Inherently optimistic about human nature, he learned to translate his sturdy cheerfulness into thousands of individual friendships spanning geography, time, and all rungs of the social ladder. His contacts ranged from president to newsboy. Brown's little secret was that he knew what made each one tick.

Hardships his mother had suffered prompted in Claude Brown a deep, lifelong interest in helping those who needed help. His experiences during the Depression turned him toward the Democratic Party. Concern for "the little man" — the great and historic hope of America — was the core of his personal philosophy.

Making friends was an art form for Claude. "I drove across the state with C. W. several years ago," recalled W. K. Ramsey of San Angelo. "In every town he knew a banker to call, and at every gas station he bought a newspaper. I drove and he read."

"I would say Claude was conspicuous for his loyalty, to his friends and to the Democratic Party," said Senator J. P. Word. Both Senator Phil Gramm and President George Bush urged George Brown to switch to the Republican Party. Brown refused to leave the Democratic Party.

Midland lawyer Maurice R. Bullock recalled Brown's political activity at the national level:

> When John F. Kennedy and Lyndon Johnson were campaigning in Texas for president and vice president in 1960, Lyndon convinced Kennedy that they should visit with Claude

Brown, who was then well-recognized as the leading Democrat in West Texas. They were traveling by airplane and organizing airport rallies. When they found that there was no airport or landing strip at McCamey sufficient to accommodate their plane, Claude arranged to have the proposed McCamey rally moved westward to Fort Stockton and its adequate airport. The Fort Stockton rally was well attended, and between Claude and Lyndon, they were able to introduce nearly everyone in attendance to then Senator John F. Kennedy, whom Lyndon called Jack.[2]

Brown gibed his friends who changed political parties: "The first two things a Democrat oil man does when he gets a good well is first to buy himself a Rolex wristwatch, then join the Republican party."

C. W. Brown did neither. Loyalty was his long suit. He was married to his wife Christine for sixty-one years, until she died of cancer. He claimed McCamey as home from the day he arrived there in 1935. His allegiance to the Democratic Party was a lifelong affair. In his later years, his list of personal friendships included some that went back to the 1920s.

CHAPTER THIRTEEN

The Other Mr. McCamey

It had to happen sooner or later. The master of ceremonies said it, his voice rising in crescendo: "And now, ladies and gentlemen, it is my pleasure to present Mr. McCamey from Brown, Texas."

Claude Brown stood up and bowed. The emcee's slip of the tongue expressed a figurative, if not a literal, truth. From that day on, Claude Brown was known as Mr. McCamey.

There was another Mr. McCamey: George B. McCamey, the wildcatter who discovered the huge pool of oil beneath the arid tableland of Upton County.

The other Mr. McCamey had a town named for him. Claude Brown in his later years was named for a town.

George B. McCamey's adventurous life began in the little town of Ridgeway (Elk County), Pennsylvania, on November 11, 1882. Forty-three years later he struck oil on a location so isolated that it was forty miles from the nearest supply point.

The M. L. Baker No. 1 was four miles from a railroad line and forty miles west of Texon. Fuel oil used to operate the well's machinery was shipped in tank cars to a rail point four miles distant; from there it was hauled by truck to the well site.

McCamey negotiated with the old Orient Railroad (no longer in operation) for a siding to be built in order for materials to be shipped by rail, switched to the siding, and unloaded from there. Because the goods going to the well were addressed to "McCamey," this surname became the unofficial name for the settlement of a few tents scattered around the railhead. The name stuck.

George B., a drilling contractor operating out of Fort Worth, had followed the classic road to success in the early days of the oil business: keep putting holes in the ground, and follow your hunches.

The hunch that paid off in Upton County stemmed from a chance meeting in a railroad car rolling across West Texas. McCamey happened to be in a car with Col. Arthur Stillwell, railroad tycoon and builder of the Orient Railroad.

The conversation turned to oil. Before many revolutions of the wheels, Stillwell convinced George McCamey that the geology of the ground over which they were rolling indicated the existence of petroleum reserves. He cited facts gathered by the English geologists and engineers who had made the original surveys for the Orient Railroad.

McCamey joined forces with another Fort Worth oil operator, Gilbert Johnson. They acquired a block of several thousand acres in Upton County in exchange for drilling a test well. Next they sold some of their leases to finance drilling costs.

When M. L. Baker No. 1 came in at a depth of 2,056 feet, McCamey and Johnson sold it for half a million dollars to Republic Production Company of Houston. Thus they had both funds and acreage left on which to drill. George B. McCamey continued to operate in the Permian Basin.

Like most individuals who succeed in the oil business, McCamey had traveled a long road with several detours before realizing his ambition. He left home at fifteen to work in Pittsburgh. His father, a millwright, appears to have been an understanding parent. "George," he explained gently, "has this little problem with train whistles."

Spindletop's stupendous yield in 1901 circulated to the farthest reaches of the country. George B. McCamey took to the road, an oil man by instinct. He made stops in Kansas, Illinois, Kentucky, Oklahoma, Utah, South Dakota, Wisconsin, and Montana while progressing from roustabout to driller to tool dresser.

In 1918 McCamey arrived at Fort Worth. He established a home and maintained an office there forty years. With several "strings of tools," he operated as a drilling contractor, mostly in the Permian Basin.

Although McCamey, the eponym, never made his home in

McCamey, the town that honored him eponymously, he liked to visit there, particularly at civic birthday celebrations and reunions.

George B. McCamey was an organizer, and later president, of the Cordova Union Oil Corporation. He served in this capacity from 1934 until 1943, when Cordova Union was sold to the Atlantic Refining Company, now Atlantic Richfield Company.

The first Mr. McCamey was a workaholic — no hobbies, just business — until he reached middle age and discovered the joy of raising thoroughbred horses. His Tarrant County showplace farm was located ten miles north of Arlington Downs, where horses raced in the 1930s. Until World War II, horses carrying the green and white silks of Bedford Stock Farm raced at the major U.S. tracks, from Santa Anita to the East Coast, from Chicago to Mexico City. McCamey shipped his stable to Mexico to race at the Hipodromo de Las Americas. He sold the stable in 1945.

Having a town named after him was very satisfying to George B. McCamey. He was proud of the fact that those who made their permanent homes there chose to keep his name for their town. When McCamey died in June 1960, the town held a memorial service for him at the site of the discovery well. His funeral service was conducted simultaneously at University Christian Church in Fort Worth.

McCamey, Texas, is almost unique in one respect: it had absolutely no reason for existence, except for the presence of large deposits of oil beneath the surface. Another Texas boomtown, Borger, was created solely by and for the oil industry. Had the wildcatters not done their work so well, both towns today would be blank spaces on the map of Texas.

The town of McCamey has one indisputable claim to fame: it is the site of a world-famous hole in the ground, a hole that has no use whatsoever.

When oil production began during the first quarter of the century, there was no place to put the precious black gold. Baker No. 1 created a tidal wave of new oil — and no place for it. Storage was a major problem. Some surface tanks had been built, most of them in California.

Shell Oil Company began work on a million-barrel oil tank. Newspaper accounts indicate it took eighteen months to build, cost $5 million, and caused five deaths. Ninety carloads of lumber were required for the covering ninety-six feet above the cement floor.

Like other experiments in business, the tank seemed to be a good idea at the time. Unfortunately, the tank leaked. It was drained and repaired twice, but the leaking continued. The million-barrel tank was finally abandoned.

McCamey was incorporated in 1927. It witnessed an engaging variety of high life and low life through the years.

Both Nelson Rockefeller and his brother Winthrop worked in the McCamey oil fields during summer vacation. The town's standard dwelling at that time was still the shotgun house — two or three rooms of one-by-twelve-inch siding, the spaces between the boards covered on the outside with thin strips of lumber. Tin roofs and linoleum floors provided finishing touches. Wind and sand blew through the houses, gusts of wind occasionally lifting the linoleum from the floor. Toilets, of course, were outside.

McCamey's main problem was water, or lack of it. Water was shipped in from Alpine at one dollar a barrel, five cents for a glass of water in a cafe.

Capt. Harry Odneal, Texas Ranger, was assigned to keep order in McCamey. The jail consisted of a post set in concrete, to which lawbreakers were chained.

Greasewood flats looked "wunnerful" to Lawrence Welk. After McCamey's discovery well in 1925 and the opening of the Yates Field in 1926, two popular taverns were T & P in McCamey and El Jardin in Rankin. The crash of 1929 had left Lawrence Welk stranded in Dallas, his band having scattered and fled. He went to Abilene, found a Model-T and a piano and two more soloists, and headed for McCamey. He stayed in the Bender Hotel and played at T&P Tavern and El Jardin.

Welk found McCamey pretty rough. He learned to hide behind his piano when a shooting scrape or a fist fight erupted over a pretty woman.

Welk courted a brunette from Rankin and wanted to marry her. One moonlit night on King's Mountain she looked at Mr. Wunnerful and said, "It makes no difference to me what your religion is, just as long as you are not a Catholic." The romance ended.

Welk refers to his second start in McCamey as having been in the "Baptist Bible Belt" of Texas.

A Dallas physician credits a gift from McCamey's Claude Brown with starting him on his career in medicine. Dr. Lorenzo

Spratt, forty-six, was a member of the last graduating class of the segregated Dunbar High School in McCamey in 1965. (The next year's class was integrated into McCamey High School.)

Lorenzo Spratt won the Texas state typing championship for high school students in April 1962 after practicing two hours a day, five days a week, for six months. When he returned from the state contest he was presented a new typewriter by Brown.

"I expect I am the first young black person to come out of McCamey to become a doctor," Spratt said in 1993. "I like to think that C. W. Brown and I are kindred spirits; we both like to achieve."

Dr. Spratt graduated from Prairie View A&M with a degree in chemistry. He did graduate work in chemistry at Baylor University before going to medical school.

In September 1970, Francis W. Dalgleish wiped away his tears in McCamey. The medical student, assuming persona and credentials of a doctor he had known in Anchorage, had practiced medicine in McCamey several weeks. However, his incorrect pronunciation of "anesthesia" aroused the suspicion that led to his exposure. Several hundred West Texans contributed to help him make bond on criminal charges and return to Australia, where doctors said Dalgleish would die due to kidney malfunction.

Lewis Ketchum traveled the Permian Basin in the 1960s representing Bethlehem Supply Company, a long way from Bartlesville, Oklahoma. Ketchum, a full-blooded Delaware Indian, met Brown on a sales trip to McCamey. Brown, with his instinct for competence and his empathy with the underdog, became interested in Ketchum. He encouraged his Indian friend to set up his own business, and helped him secure the financing to get started.

Red Man Supply Company in Tulsa today is a full-service oil field and industrial supply company with thirty-nine branches and 270 employees. President Reagan in 1987 honored Ketchum as "Minority Entrepreneur of the Year."

When Claude and Nova Brown visited Tulsa in 1993, Lew Ketchum offered them a private performance of Delaware tribal dancing.

Claude liked to quote Proverbs 28:27:

> He who gives to the poor will not want, but he who hides his eye shall get many a curse.

CHAPTER FOURTEEN

August 9, 1993

"As long as I live," Brown told his friends, "I will live in West Texas, doing what I can to promote it. When I do leave, it will be when my Maker says, 'Well done, my good and faithful servant. We have some exploring and promoting for you to do in a new world.'"

Claude Brown was slipping away, his family near, his heartbeat weaker and weaker.

Harry and Mary Spannus, friends from the Permian Basin Petroleum Association, walked into the hospital room.

"Claude," Harry mocked an exasperated tone. "You've lost more of these Top Hand awards than anybody else in West Texas has even looked at. We decided to make one for you that you'll have trouble losing." Harry held up a solid copper likeness of Claude Brown, tribute to an industry pioneer who looked inward rather than outward for his destiny.

Claude had enjoyed the struggle and its abundant honors. He had walked with presidents and paupers. He had drilled more than 500 wells. He belonged to the Hall of Fame of the Permian Basin Petroleum Museum. He was Mr. McCamey, Mr. West Texas, Mr. Democrat. He could walk down the street in any Texas town and see someone he called friend. The Top Hand award was the icing on the cake.

Claude, like Odysseus, had battled the varied storms of life and won.

He reached out for the Top Hand.

Nice Guys Do Finish First

The twentieth century has been the hydrocarbon age. The lifespan of Claude Wilson Brown was congruent with the tumultuous rise of the industry that became the dominant economic factor in the state of Texas.

Because of their dynamic nature and instant-wealth potential, the oil fields and their people have fascinated those who live and work outside the industry. A stereotypical view of oil men as hustlers, opportunists, and con artists permeates many areas of society. The gamy side of boomtowns is well known in an age that finds little about the past that is satisfactory.

Men who built the oil business had to be tough, self-reliant, resourceful, and tireless. They had to take risks and take the consequences. They had to make the most of each situation. Success, however, did not equate with lack of ethics.

The authors of this book knew Claude Brown for forty years. We believe his life illustrates that nice guys do finish first. The way Claude Brown used and shared his blessings is an inspiration to us. We hope it will be for others.

Notes

Chapter One

1. Bernard deVoto, *The Course of Empire* (Boston: Houghton-Mifflin, 1952), 272.
2. *Ibid.*, 273.
3. T. R. Fehrenbach, *Lone Star* (New York: Macmillan, 1968), 92.
4. Cran and MacNeil McCrum, *The Story of English* (New York: Viking, 1986), 156.
5. John H. Pope, ed., *John Berry and His Children* (Georgetown: John Berry Associates, 1988), 11ff.
6. *Ibid.*, 351.

Chapter Two

1. T. R. Fehrenbach, *Seven Keys to Texas* (El Paso: Texas Western Press, 1983), 43.
2. Emily Dickinson, "XIII," *Poems by Emily Dickinson*, edited by Martha Dickinson Bianchi and Alfred Leete Hampson (Boston: Little, Brown, 1956).
3. Richard R. Moore, *West Texas After the Discovery of Oil* (Austin: Jenkins, 1971), 24.

Chapter Three

1. Richard R. Moore, *West Texas After the Discovery of Oil* (Austin: Jenkins, 1971), 24.

Chapter Six

1. Samuel D. Myres, interview with Willie and Anna Wolf, McCamey, Texas, February 1970.

Chapter Eleven

1. J. C. Furnas, *The Americans* (New York: Putnam, 1969), 247.

2. S. E. Morison and H. S. Commager, *The Growth of the American Republic* (New York: Oxford University Press, 1952), 243.

3. Olin W. Nail, *The First 100 Years 1858–1958* (The Southwest Texas Conference of the Methodist Church. Austin: Capital Printing Co., 1958), 24.

4. J. Evetts Haley, *Men of Fiber*, Shamrock edition (Amarillo: Shamrock, 1963), 26.

Chapter Twelve

1. Peggy N. Nash, interview with Maurice R. Bullock in Midland, Texas, February 1994.

2. *Ibid.*

Bibliography

Ball, Max W., Douglas Ball, and Daniel S. Turner. *This Fascinating Oil Business*. Indianapolis: Bobbs-Merrill Company, 1965.

Boorstin, D. J. *The Americans: The National Experience*. New York: Random House, 1965.

Brantly, J. E. *History of Oil Well Drilling*. Houston: Gulf Publishing Company, 1971.

Clark, James A., and Michael T. Halbouty. *The Last Boom*. New York: Random House, 1972.

DeVoto, Bernard. *The Course of Empire*. Boston: Houghton-Mifflin Company, 1952.

Eagleton, N. Ethie. *On the Last Frontier: A History of Upton County, Texas*. El Paso: Texas Western Press, University of Texas at El Paso, 1971.

Fehrenbach, T. R. *Lone Star – A History of Texas and the Texans*. New York: Macmillan Publishing Company, Inc., 1968.

———. *Seven Keys to Texas*. El Paso: Texas Western Press, 1983.

Garraty, John A. *The Age of the Great Depression*. New York: Harcourt Brace Jovanovich, 1986.

Haley, J. Evetts. *Men of Fiber*. Amarillo: Shamrock Oil Company, 1963.

Lampasas County Historical Commission. *Lampasas County Texas – Its History and Its People*. Marceline: Walsworth Publishing Company, 1991.

Mallison, Sam T. *The Great Wildcatter: The Story of Mike Benedum*. Charleston: Education Foundation of West Virginia, Inc., 1953.

Moore, Richard R. *West Texas After the Discovery of Oil: A Modern Frontier*. Austin and New York: The Pemberton Press, 1971.

Morison, Samuel E., and Henry S. Commager. *The Growth of the American Republic*. New York: Oxford University Press, 1962.

91

Myres, Samuel D. *The Permian Basin – Petroleum Empire of the Southwest.* 2 vols. El Paso: Permian Press, 1975.

Olien, Roger M., and Diana Davids. *Wildcatters: Texas Independent Oilmen.* Austin: Texas Monthly Press, 1984.

Poe, Charlsie. *Runnels is My County.* San Antonio: The Naylor Company, 1970.

Pope, John H., ed. *John Berry and His Children.* Georgetown: John Berry Associates, 1988.

Rae, John B. *The American Automobile.* Chicago: The University of Chicago Press, 1965.

Stern, Philip Van Doren. *Tin Lizzie.* New York: Simon and Schuster, 1955.

Wecter, Dixon. *The Age of the Great Depression 1929–1941.* New York: Macmillan Company, 1948.

Welk, Lawrence (with Bernice McGeehan). *Wunnerful, Wunnerful.* Englewood Cliffs: Prentice-Hall, Inc., 1971.

Yergin, Daniel. *The Prize.* New York: Simon and Schuster, 1991.

Index

93